The PEBL Manual
Programming and Usage Guide for
The Psychology Experiment Building Language
PEBL Version 0.13

Shane T. Mueller

Current for PEBL Version 0.13 – September 2012
http://pebl.sourceforge.net

Contents

About the Author

Shane T. Mueller received his Ph.D. in Cognitive Psychology from the University of Michigan. His research interests cover a broad range, but usually involve mathematical, computational, or statistical modeling of human behavior at an individual or group level. Furthermore, his work has sought to be integrative and incorporate broad measures of human intelligence and cognition.

After receiving his Ph.D. under the direction of David E. Meyer, he conducted post-doctoral research under the supervision of Richard Shiffrin at Indiana University, where he studied human semantic and perceptual representation, learning, and decision making. Following this, he moved to Klein Associates Division of Applied Research Associates, where he developed the Bayesian Recognitional Decision Model, the BICA Cognitive Decathlon (an embodied version of the Turing Test), Cultural Mixture Modeling (a method for identifying shared beliefs and disagreements in groups), and the C2T3 approach for measuring and modeling cognitive impairment from physiological stressors. In 2011, he joined Michigan Technological University as a member of the Department of Cognitive and Learning Sciences. He lives in Houghton, Michigan.

Chapter 1

About

PEBL (Psychology Experiment Building Language) is a cross-platform, open-source programming language and execution environment for constructing programs to conduct a wide range of archetypal psychology experiments. It is entirely free of charge, and may be modified to suit your needs as long as you follow the terms of the GPL, under which the source code is licensed. PEBL is written primarily in C++, but requires a few other tools (flex, yacc) and libraries (SDL, SDL_image, SDL_gfx, and SDL_ttf) to use. In addition, a set of audio recording functions are available using the (now old and basically unmaintained) sdl_audioin library. Finally, the waave library optionally supports movie playback on linux and windows.

It currently compiles and runs on Linux (using g++), Mac OSX (using xcode), and Microsoft Windows (using code:blocks and mingw) platforms using free tools. It has been developed primarily by Shane T. Mueller, Ph.D. (smueller@obereed.net). This document was prepared with editorial and formatting help from Gulab Parab and Samuele Carcagno. Contributions are welcome and encouraged.

Chapter 2

Usage

Most users will be able to download a precompiled version of PEBL and run experiments directly. Some advanced users may wish to compile their own version, however. The next section describes how to do this.

2.1 How to Compile

Currently, there is no automated compile procedure. PEBL requires the SDL, SDL-image, SDL-gfx SDL_net, SDL_audioin and SDL-ttf libraries and development headers. It also uses `flex` and `bison`, but you can compile without these tools. PEBL compiles on both Linux and Windows using the free `gcc` compiler; on windows this is most easily supported through the code:blocks IDE. Note that SDL-image may require `jpeg`, `png`, and a `zlib` compression library, while SDL-ttf uses `truetype` 2.0.

2.1.1 Linux

PEBL should compile by typing 'make' in its base directory once all requisite tools are installed and the source distribution is uncompressed. Currently, PEBL does not use autotools, so its make system is rather brittle. Assistance is welcome.

On Linux, compiling will fail if you don't have an /obj directory and all the appropriate subdirectories (that mirror the main tree.) These will not exist if you check out from CVS.

2.1.2 Microsoft Windows

On Microsoft Windows, PEBL is designed to be compiled using the Free IDE `code:blocks`. A code:blocks project file is included in the source code directory. Email the PEBL list for more details.

2.1.3   Mac OSX

Originally, PEBL compiled to a command-line function. Since 0.12, PEBL will compile to a .app package using xcode. An xcode package is available in the source package.

2.2   Installation

2.2.1   Linux

On Linux, there are .deb packages available for debian. However, it is fairly easy to compile and install from source. To begin, be sure that all the sdl packages are installed. Then, go to the main pebl directory and type:

```
>make
>sudo make install
```

Once installed, you can install the test battery into `Documents/pebl-exp.X` using the command pebl –install.

2.2.2   Microsoft Windows

In Microsoft Windows, we provide an installer package that contains all necessary executable binary files and `.dlls`. This installer places PEBL in `c:\Program Files\PEBL`, and creates a directory `pebl-exp.X` in `My Documents` with a shortcut that allows PEBL to be launched and programs that reside there to be run.

2.2.3   Macintosh OSX

For OSX, we provide a `.app` package that can be dragged into your Applications folder. The first time any user runs pebl, it gives the option to install the battery and other files into Documentspebl-exp.X. Afterward, it will run the launcher from that directory.

2.3   How to Run a PEBL Program

The simplest way to run any PEBL script is via the launcher, which is available on all platforms. The launcher is covered in detail in Chapter 6. But, you can also launch experiments individually on each platform.

2.3.1   Linux

If you have installed PEBL into `/usr/local/bin`, you will be able to invoke PEBL by typing 'pebl' at a command line. PEBL requires you to specify one or more source files that it will compile and run, e.g., the command:

```
> pebl stroop.pbl library.pbl
```

will load the experiment described in `stroop.pbl`, and will load the supplementary library functions in `library.pbl`.

Additionally, PEBL can take the -v or -V command-line parameter, which allows you to pass values into the script. This is useful for entering subject numbers and condition types using an outside program like a bash script (possibly one that invokes dialog or zenity). A sample zenity script that asks for subject number and then runs a sample experiment which uses that input resides in the `bin` directory. The script can be edited to use fullscreen mode or change the display dimensions, for example. See Section 2.3.3: Command-Line Arguments. You can also specify directories without a filename on the command-line (as long as they end with '/'). Doing so will add that directory to the search path when files are opened.

2.3.2 Microsoft Windows

PEBL can be launched from the command line in Windows by going to the `pebl\bin` directory and typing 'pebl.exe'. PEBL requires you to specify one or more source files that it will compile and run. For example, the command

```
> pebl.exe stroop.pbl library.pbl
```

loads the experiment described in `stroop.pbl`, and loads supplementary library functions in `library.pbl`.

Additionally, PEBL can take the -v or -V command-line parameter, which allows you to pass values in to the script. This is useful for entering condition types using an outside program like a batch file. the -s and -S allow one to specify a subject code, which gets bound to the gSubNum variable. If no value is specified, gSubNum is initialized to 0. You can also specify directories without a file (as long as they end with '\'). Doing so will add that directory to the search path when files are opened. See Section 2.3.3: Command-Line Arguments.

Launching programs from the command-line on Windows is cumbersome. One easy way to launch PEBL on Windows is to create a shortcut to the executable file and then edit the properties so that the shortcut launches PEBL with the proper script and command-line parameters. Another way is to write and launch a batch file, which is especially useful if you wish to enter configuration data before loading the script.

2.3.3 Macintosh OSX

The latest version of PEBL packaged for OSX is 0.12. It is compiled as an application bundle with both 32-bit and 64-bit architectures available. We do not support PPC architecture.

The simplest way to run PEBL is through the launcher, but you can also use Applescript to create your own sequences of experiments.

On OSX, PEBL can be run as a command-line tool, just as in linux. Once installed, the application is located at /Applications/pebl.app/Contents/MacOS/pebl.

2.4   How to stop running a program

In order to improve performance, PEBL runs at the highest priority possible on your computer. This means that if it gets stuck somewhere, you may have difficulty terminating the process. We have added an 'abort program' shortcut key combination that will immediately terminate the program and report the location at which it became stuck in your code:
press <CTRL><SHIFT><ALT><\> simultaneously.

2.5   Command-line arguments

Some aspects of PEBL's display can be controlled via command-line arguments. Some of these are platform specific, or their use depends on your exact hardware and software. The following guide to command-line arguments is adapted from the output produced by invoking PEBL with no arguments:

Usage: Invoke PEBL with the experiment script files (.pbl) and command-line arguments.

Examples:
```
pebl experiment.pbl -s sub1 --fullscreen --display 800x600
      --driver dga
pebl experiment.pbl --driver xf86   --language es
pebl experiment.pbl -v 33 -v 2 --fullscreen --display 640x480
```

Command-Line Options

-v VALUE1 -v VALUE2

> Invokes script and passes VALUE1 and VALUE2 (or any text immediately following a -v) to a list in the argument of the Start() function.
> This is useful for passing in conditions, subject numbers, randomization cues, and other entities that are easier to control from outside the script. Variables appear as strings, so numeric values need to be converted to be used as numbers.

 -s VALUE
   -S VALUE

> Binds VALUE to the global variable gSubNum, which is set by default to 0.

--driver <drivername>

> Sets the video driver, when there is more than one. In Linux SDL, options xf86, dga, svgalib (from console), itcan also be controlled via environment variables. In fact, for SDL versions of PEBL simply set the

SDL_VIDEO_DRIVER environment variable to the passed-in argument, without doing any checking, and without checking or returning it to its original state.

--display <widthxheight>

Controls the screen width and height (in pixels). Defaults to the current resolution of the screen. Unlike older versions of PEBL, after 0.12 any legal combination of width and height should work.

The screensize a PEBL script runs at depends on a number of things. If no –display size is given (e.g., when 'default' is chosen in the launcher), PEBL will try to determine the current screen size and use that, for both fullscreen and windowed mode. Otherwise, it will try to use the specified value.

However, these values are only a request. When the script starts, it sets the values of the global variables gVideoWidth and gVideoHeight based on either the specified values or the current screen size. These values can be changed in the script before the MakeWindow function is called, so that a script can require a particular screen size. Then, the window will be created with those dimensions, overriding any command-line parameters. For greatest flexibility, it is recommended that you do not hard-code screen size but rather make your test adapt to a large number of screen sizes.

Finally, if a screen size is selected that the video card cannot support (i.e., in fullscreen mode), gVideWidth and gVideoHeight will be set to the legal screen size closest to the one you requested. PEBL should never crash because you have specified the wrong screen size, but it should rather use one it can support. The values of gVideoWidth and gVideoHeight will be changed by MakeWindow to whatever screen size it actually uses.

--depth

Controls the pixel depth, which also depends on your video card. Currently, depths of 2,8,15,16,24, and 32 are allowed on the command-line. There is no guarantee that you will get the specified bit depth, and bit depths such as 2 and 8 are likely never useful. Changing depths can, for some drivers and video cards, enable better performance or possibly better video sychrony. Defaults to 32.

--language

Allows user to specify a language code that can get tested for within a script to select proper translation. It sets a global variable gLanguage, and is "en" by default.

--windowed or **--fullscreen** Controls whether the script will run in a window or fullscreen. The screen resolution a PEBL script runs at depends on a number of things. See the **--display** option above for more details.

Chapter 3

How to Write a PEBL Program

3.1 Basic PEBL Scripts

PEBL has a fairly straightforward and forgiving syntax, and implements most of its interesting functionality in a large object system and function library of over 125 functions. The library includes many functions specific to creating and presenting stimuli and collecting responses. Efforts, however successful, have been made to enable timing accuracy at amillisecond-scale, and to make machine limitations easy to deal with.

Each PEBL program is stored in a text file. Currently, no special authoring environment is available. A program consists of one or more functions, and *must* have a function called `Start()`. Functions are defined with the following syntax:

```
define <function_name>(parameters)
{
  statement 1
  statement 2
  ....
  return value3
}
```

The parameter list and the return value are optional. For the `Start(par){}` function, `par` is normally bound to 0. However, if PEBL is invoked with `-v` command-line parameters, each value that follows a `-v` is added to a list contained in 'par', which can then be accessed within the program:

11

```
define Start(par)
{
    Print(First(par))
}
```

A simple PEBL program that actually runs follows:

```
define Start(par)
{
 Print("Hello")
}
```

`Print()` is a standard library function. If you run PEBL from a command-line, the text inside the `Print` function will be sent to the console. On Windows, it will appear in the file 'stdout.txt' in the PEBL directory. Although other functions do not need a parameter argument, the `Start()` function does (case values are passed in from the command-line).

A number of sample PEBL programs can be found in the /demo subdirectory.

3.2   Case Sensitivity

PEBL uses case to specify an item's token type. This serves as an extra contextual cue to the programmer, so that the program reads more easily and communicates more clearly.

Function names must start with an uppercase letter, but are otherwise case-insensitive. Thus, if you name a function "DoTrial", you can call it later as "DOTRIAL" or "Dotrial" or even "DotRail". We recommend consistency, as it helps manage larger programs more easily.

Unlike function names, variable names must start with an lowercase letter; if this letter is a 'g', the variable is global. This enforces a consistent and readable style. After the first character, variable names are caseinsensitive. Thus, the variable 'mytrial' is the same as 'myTrial'.

Currently, syntax keywords (like loop, if, define, etc.) must be lowercase, for technical reasons. We hope to eliminate this limitation in the future.

3.3   Syntax

PEBL has a simple and forgiving syntax, reminiscent of S+ (or R) and c. However, differences do exist.

Table 3.1 shows a number of keywords and symbols used in PEBL. These need not appear in lowercase in your program.

Note that the '=' symbol does not exist in PEBL. Unlike other languages, PEBL does not use it as an assignment operator. Instead, it uses '<-'. Because it is confusing for users to keep track of the various uses of the = and == symbols, we've eliminated the '=' symbol entirely. Programmers familiar with c will notice a resemblance between PEBL and c. Unlike c, in PEBL a semicolon is not necessary to finish a statement. A carriage return indicates a statement is

Table 3.1: PEBL Symbols and Keywords

Symbol/Keyword	Usage
+	Adds two expressions together
-	Subtracts one expression from another
/	Divides one expression by another
*	Multiplies two expressions together
^	Raises one expression to the power of another
;	Finishes a statement, or starts a new statement on the same line (is not needed at end of line)
.	The property accessor. Allows properties to be accessed by name
<-	The assignment operator
( )	Groups mathematical operations
{ }	Groups a series of statements
[ ]	Creates a list
#	Comment—ignore everything on the line that follows
<	Less than
>	Greater than
<=	Less than or equal to
>=	Greater than or equal to
==	Equal to
<> != ~=	Not equal to
and	Logical and
break	Breaks out of a loop prematurely
not	Logical not
or	Logical or
while	Traditional while loop
loop	Loops over elements in a list
if	Simple conditional test
if...else	Complex conditional test
if...elseif...else	Extended conditional chain
define	Defines a function
return	Allows a function to return a value

complete, if the current line forms a complete expression. You may terminate every command with a ';' if you choose, but it may slow down parsing and execution.

Another difference between c and PEBL is that in PEBL, {} brackets are not optional: they are required to define code blocks, such as those found in `if` and `while` statements and loops.

3.4   Expressions

An expression is a set of operations that produces a result. In PEBL, every function is an expression, as is any single number. Expressions include:

```
3 + 32
(324 / 324) - Log(32)
not lVariable
Print(32323)
"String " + 33
nsuho  #this is legal if nsuho has been defined already.
```

Notice that `"String "  33+` is a legal expresison. It will produce another string: `"String 33"`.

These are not expressions:

```
NSUHO        #Not an expression
( 33 + 33    #Not an expression
444 / 3342 + #Not an expression
```

`NSUHO` is not a variable because it starts with a capital letter. The other lines are incomplete expressions. If the PEBL parser comes to the end of a line with an incomplete expression, it will automatically go to the next line:

```
Print("hello " +
      " world."
    )
```

This can result in bugs that are hard to diagnose:

```
a <- 33 + 323 +
Print(1331)
```

sets `a` to the string `"3561331"`.

But if a carriage return occurs at a point where the line does make a valid expression, it will treat that line as a complete statement:

```
a <- 33 + 323
 * 34245
```

sets a equal to 356, but creates a syntax error on the next line.

Any expression can be used as the argument of a function, but a function may not successfully operate when given bogus arguments.

If a string is defined across line breaks, the string definition will contain a linebreak character, which will get printed in output text files and textboxes.

```
text <- "this is a line
and so is this"
```

If you desire a long body of text without linebreaks, you must define it piecemeal:

```
text <- "This is a line " +
        "There is no line break before this line."
```

3.5 Variables

PEBL can store the results of expressions in named variables. Unlike many programming languages, PEBL only has one type of variable: a "Variant". This variable type can hold strings, integers, floating-point numbers, lists, graphical objects, and everything else PEBL uses to create an experiment. Unlike other languages, a variable need not be declared before it can be used. If you try to access a variable that has not yet been declared, PEBL will return a fatal error that stipulates as such.

3.5.1 Coercion/casting

Variants just hide the representational structure from the user. An actual string resides within the variant that holds a string. A long integer resides within the variant that holds an integer.

PEBL Variants are automatically coerced or cast to the most appropriate inner format. For example, 3232.2 + 33 starts out as a floating point and an integer. The sum is cast to a floating point number. Similarly, "banana" + 33 starts as a string and an integer, but the combination is a string.

3.5.2 Variable Naming

All variables must begin with a lowercase letter. Any sequence of numbers or letters may follow that letter. If the variable begins with a lowercase 'g', it has global scope; otherwise it has local scope.

3.5.3 Variable Scope

As described above, variables can have either local or global scope. Any variable with global scope is accessible from within any function in your program. A variable with local scope is accessible only from within its own function. Different functions can have local variables with the same name. Generally, it is a good idea to use local variables whenever possible, but using global variables for graphical objects and other complex data types can be intuitive.

3.5.4 Copies and Assignment

Variables may contain various types of data, such as simple types like integers, floating-point ratio numbers, strings; and complex types like lists, windows, sounds, fonts, etc. A variable can be set to a new value, but by design, there are very few ways in which a complex object can be changed once it has been set. For example:

```
woof    <- LoadSound("dog.wav")
meow    <- LoadSound("cat.wav")
dog     <- woof
```

Notice that woof and dog refer to the same sound object. Now you may:

```
PlayBackground(woof)
Wait(50)
Stop(dog)
```

which will stop the sound from playing. If instead you:

```
PlayBackground(woof)
Wait(50)
Stop(meow)
```

woof will play until it is complete or the program ends.
Images provide another example. Suppose you create and add an image to a window:

```
mWindow <- MakeWindow()
mImage  <- MakeImage("test.bmp")
AddObject(mImage, mWindow)
Draw()
```

Now, suppose you create another variable and assign its value to `mImage`:

```
mImage2 <- mImage
Move(mImage2, 200, 300)
Draw()
```

Even though `mImage2` was never added to `mWindow`, `mImage` has moved: different variables now point to the same object. Note that this does not happen for simple (non-object) data types:

```
a <- 33
b <- a
a <- 55
Print(a + "   " + b)
```

This produces the output:

```
55   33
```

This may seem confusing at first, but the consistency pays off in time. The '<-' assignment operator never changes the value of the data attached to a variable, it just changes what the variable points to. PEBL is functional in its handling of simple data types, so you can't, for example, directly modify the contents of a string.

```
a  <- "my string"     #assigns a string literal to a
b  <- a               #makes b refer to a's string literal
a  <- "your string"   #re-assigns a to a new string literal
b  <- a               #makes b refer to a's new string literal
```

3.5.5 Passing by Reference and by Value

The discussion in 3.5.4 on copying has implications for passing variables into functions. When a variable is passed into a function, PEBL makes a copy of that variable on which to operate. But, as discussed in 3.5.4, if the variable holds a complex data type (object or a list), the primary data structure allows for direct modification. This is practical: if you pass a window into a function, you do not want to make a copy of that window on which to operate. If the value is a string or a number, a copy of that value is made and passed into the function.

3.6   Functions

The true power of PEBL lies in its extensive library of functions that allow specific experiment-related tasks to be accomplished easily. For the sake of convenience, the library is divided into a number of subordinate libraries. This library structure is transparent to the user, who does not need to know where a function resides in order to use it. Chapter 5 includes a quick reference to functions; Chapter 8 includes a complete alphabetical reference.

3.7   A Simple Program

The previous sections provide everything you need to know to write a simple program. Here is an annotated program:

```
# Any line starting with a # is a comment.  It gets ignored.


#Every program needs to define a function called Start()
#Start always needs a parameter
define Start(par)
{

 number <- 10    ##Assign a number to a variable

 hello  <- "Hello World"  ##Assign a string to a variable
 ##Create a global variable (starts with little g)
 gGlobalText <- "Global Text"

 ##Call a user-defined function (defined below).
 value <-  PrintIt(hello, number)
 ##It returned a value
 #Call a built-in function
 Print("Goodbye. " + value)
}

##Define a function with two variables.
define PrintIt(text, number)
{
  #Seed RNG with the current time.
  RandomizeTimer()
  #Generate a random number between 1 and number
  i <- RandomDiscrete(number)   #this is a built-in function
  ##Create a counter variable
  j <- 0
  ##Keep sampling until we get the number we chose.
  while(i != number)
  {
      Print(text + "   " + i + gGlobalText)
      i <- RandomDiscrete(number)
      j <- j + 1
  }

  return(j)  #return the counter variable.
}
```

More sample programs can be found in the **demo/** and **experiments/** directories of the PEBL source tree.

18

Chapter 4

Overview of Object Subsystems

In PEBL, complex objects are stored and automatically self-managed. These objects include lists, graphical display widgets like images and text displays, fonts, colors, audio files, and input or output files. Objects are created and modified with special functions, but many of their properties available directly for access and modification with a `variable.property` syntax. For example, the position of a textbox is controlled by `.X` and `.Y` properties, and can also be changed with the `Move()` function. To move the label `lab`, which is located at 100,100, to 150,100, you can either do `Move(lab,150,100)` or `lab.X <- 150`. The available properties and accessor function are listed in the decriptions of their relevant objects below.

4.1 Lists

Lists are incredibly useful and flexible storage structures that play an important role in PEBL. A list is simply a series of variables. It is the equivalent to a vector, array, or other similar data structure in many other programming languages. Creating and accessing elements of lists can be accomplished in a number of ways. If you have a set of values you want to create a list from, you simply need to put them inside square brackets, separated by commas:

```
mylist <- [1,2,3,4,5,6,7,8,9]
```

Many functions related to experimental design return lists already created. Two simple functions are `Repeat` and `Sequence`:

```
list1 <- Repeat(0,10)      ##ten zeroes
list2 <- Sequence(0,20,2)  ##numbers 0 to 20 step 2
```

Accessing list items can be done in a number of ways. The simplest is using the `Nth()` function. For a slightly more complex example, suppose you want to print out every item in a list. Looping through, accessing, and printing all the items of a list using this approach:

```
list <- Sequence(1,9,1)
len <- Length(list)
i <- 1
while (i <= len)
 {
    item <- Nth(list,i)
    Print(item)
    i <- i + 1
}
```

Note that prior to PEBL 0.12, using Nth to access list items was inefficient. Since PEBL 0.13, you can use Nth to access list items in amortized constant time! But nevertheless, the above method of looping is verbose and error-prone. There is an alternative. Items from lists can be iterated over using the 'loop' command:

```
list <- Sequence(1,9,1)
loop(item, list)
{
   Print(item)
}
```

These two code blocks produce identical output, but in the former block, each item of the list must be found on each iteration, but in the latter block, a list item is bound directly to 'item' on each iteration. There is no appreciable difference in the efficiency of these two methods, but the second is simpler and in many cases easier to use, and avoids some errors (like forgetting to increment i).

4.1.1 Growing Lists

Oftentimes, you want to create a list one element at a time. For example, you may have a sampling scheme for stimuli and need to pick each consecutive randomly, or you want to record response times or accuracies one trial at a time. There are two ways you can do this. If you know how long your list will be, you can create a list with as many elements as you need, and then alter each element one at a time.

```
##I need ten items

items <- Repeat(0,10)
i <- 1
```

```
while(i <= Length(items))
{
  SetElement(items,i,Random())
}
```

Oftentimes, however, this is difficult because you do no know how long the list should be at the beginning. The `Append()` function is able to add an item to the end of a list, and you can use that to 'grow' a list one item at a time:

```
##I need ten items

items <- []
i <- 1
while(i <= 10)
{
  items <- Append(items,Random())
}
```

This ideom is used in many places in PEBL test batteries. However, it can be inefficient as the length of the list grows. This is because on each iteration, a new list is created that is 1 element longer than the previous list (and each element is copied to the new list). For small lists, even ones hundred of items long, this overhead is pretty small and you hardly notice. But as a list gets thousands of items long, this can start to slow things down, especially if you are doing something complex between each trial. As of PEBL 0.13, we support another function called PushOnEnd():

```
items <- []
i <- 1
while(i <= 10)
{
  PushOnEnd(items,Random())
}
```

PushOnEnd will alter `items` directly, and do so in a very efficient way. Notice that you don't need to copy the new list and overwrite itself. However, for ease of use, `PushOnEnd()` returns the current copy of the list, and so you can often use it as a drop-in replacement for Append (in cases where you are throwing away the original list). In tests, this method appears to be only 5-10% less efficient than using `PushOnEnd` alone, and so it should hardly be noticed.

```
items <- []
i <- 1
while(i <= 10)
{
  items <- PushOnEnd(items,Random())
}
```

A caveat when using lists: Some functions operate on lists to produce new lists (sub-lists, re-ordered lists, etc.). When the lists contain simple data types (numbers, strings, etc.), entirely new data structures are created. But when the data structures are complex (windows, sounds, images, etc.), the objects are not copied. Only new pointers to the original objects are created. So if you change the original object, you may end up accidentally changing the new object. Although that is relatively difficult, because PEBL allows only limited modification of existing data structures, it is still possible. This is a special case of the copy/assignment issue discussed in Section 3.5.4: Copies and Assignment.

4.1.2 Recursion on lists

Many mathematical functions that take a single argument can be applied either to a number or a list of numbers. When applied to an entire list, it will return the function applied to each element of that list. For example, `Ln(1)` return 0, but `Ln([1,1,1]` returns [0,0,0].

A list of functions that support this include:

- Log10
- Log2
- Ln
- Exp
- Sqrt
- Tan
- Sin
- Cos
- ATan
- ASin
- ACos
- DegToRad
- RadToDeg
- Round
- Floor
- Ceiling
- AbsFloor
- Sign
- Abs

In addition, a number of math functions that take two argumunts will apply themselves recursively to the first argument should it be a list. For example, `LogN([1,1,1],5)` will return [0,0,0]. Functions that support this include:

- LogN
- Pow
- NthRoot

4.2   Fonts

PEBL uses truetype fonts for the display of text in labels and other text widgets. In addition to the filename, font objects have the following properties: style (i.e., normal, bold, italic, underline), size (in points), foreground color, background color, and whether it should be rendered anti-aliased.

We distribute a series of high-quality freely available and redistributable fonts, including the DejaVu series, freefont series, and a few others. These include the typeface/files shown below 4.1:

These should always be available for use in experiments. The `fonts.pbl` script in the demo/ directory will display what symbols from each of these fonts looks like.

To use, you need only specify the font name in the `MakeFont()` function:

```
colorRed   <- MakeColor("red")
colorGrey <- MakeColor("grey")
myFont     <- MakeFont("VeraMono.ttf",0,22,colorRed,colorGrey,1)
```

This code makes a red 22-point anti-aliased font on a grey background. Other fonts may be used by specifying their absolute pathname or copying them to the working directory and using them.

Accessible font properties:

```
font.FILENAME
font.BOLD
font.UNDERLINE
font.ITALIC
font.SIZE
font.FGCOLOR
font.BGCOLOR
font.ANTIALIASED
```

Having the right fonts is important for translating PEBL scripts into new languages. Previously, this was challenging because the default font used in many scripts was Vera, and Vera has poor support for international characters. As of PEBL 0.11, a few things have changed to make international character support easier:

- Three new fonts that support international characters much better ("DejaVuSans.ttf", "DejaVuSansMono.ttf", and "DejaVuSerif.ttf") are now included and available.

- Three new global variables are set on initiation: `gPEBLBaseFont`, `gPEBLBaseFontMono`, and `gPEBLBaseFontSerif`, which are set by default to these three font names.

- Helper functions and battery tests are all updated to use these values to set up fonts.

Table 4.1: Typeface/Files Available in PEBL

Filename	Description
	FreeFont Fonts
`FreeSans.ttf`	Simple Clean sans serif font
`FreeSansBold.ttf`	
`FreeSansOblique.ttf`	
`FreeSansBoldOblique.ttf`	
`FreeMono.ttf`	Courier-like fontface
`FreeMonoBold.ttf`	
`FreeMonoOblique.ttf`	
`FreeMonoBoldOblique.ttf`	
`FreeSerif.ttf`	Similar to Times New Roman
`FreeSerifBold.ttf`	
`FreeSerifItalic.ttf`	
`FreeSerifBoldItalic.ttf`	
	Fontforge Fonts
`Caliban.ttf`	Helvetica-style
`CaslonRoman.ttf`	Quirky Roman Font series
`CaslonBold.ttf`	
`CaslonItalic.ttf`	
`Caslon-Black.ttf`	
`Humanistic.ttf`	Sharp, refined fontface
	SIL Fonts
`DoulosSILR.ttf`	Comprehensive font with roman and cyrillic glyphs
`GenR102.ttf`	Includes many latin alphabet letters
`GenI102.ttf`	
`CharisSILR.ttf`	Like doulos, optimized for printing
`CharisSILB.ttf`	
`CharisSILI.ttf`	
`CharisSILBI.ttf`	
	PEBL Fonts
`Stimulasia.ttf`	A small set of arrow/boxes
	Bitstream Vera Series (Deprecated in favor of DejaVu)
`Vera.ttf`	Sans serif Roman-style base font
`VeraMono.ttf`	Sans serif Roman-style mono-spaced base font
`VeraSe.ttf`	Serif Roman-style base font (similar to times)
`VeraBd.ttf`	Bold Vera
`VeraIt.ttf`	Italic Vera
`VeraBI.ttf`	Bold Italic Vera
`VeraMoBd.ttf`	Bold Vera Mono
`VeraMoIt.ttf`	Italic Vera Mono
`VeraMoBI.ttf`	Bold Italic Vera Mono
`VeraSeBd.ttf`	Bold Serif Vera
	DejaVu Series (Version of Vera with international characters)
`DejaVuSerif.ttf`	Serif Roman-style base font (similar to times)
`DejaVuSans.ttf`	Serif Roman-style base font
`DejaVuSansMono.ttf`	Sans serif Roman-style mono-spaced base font
	CJK Fonts
`wqy-zenhei.ttc`	All-purpose font with support for Chinese, Korean and Japanese

So now, many international characters will be handled by default. For character sets that aren't handled by DejaVu, simply needs to change `gPEBLBaseFont` to name a font that can handle your characters (and include that font in the program directory), and everything should work out fine.

4.3   Colors

Colors are PEBL objects. A color can be created by specifying its name using the `MakeColor()` function, or by specifying its RGB values using the `MakeColorRGB()` function. A list of colors and their respective RGB values can be found in the `Colors.txt` file in the documentation directory, or in the final chapter of the manual. There are nearly 800 from which to choose, so you can create just about anything you can imagine.

Accessible color properties:

```
color.RED
color.GREEN
color.BLUE
color.ALPHA
```

4.4   Windows

To run an experiment, you usually need to create a window in which to display stimuli. This is done with the `MakeWindow()` function. `MakeWindow()` will create a grey window by default, or you can specify a color. Currently, an experiment can have only one window.

4.5   Graphical Widgets

Graphical "widgets" are the building blocks of experimental stimuli. Currently, four widgets are available: images, labels, canvasses, and textboxes. More complicated widgets are in progress or planned. There are also a number of shapes that in some ways behave like widgets, but are technically not.

To be used, a widget must be created and added to a parent window, and then the parent window must be drawn. You can hide widgets with the `Hide()` function, and show them with the `Show()` function; however, this affects only the visibility of the widget: it is still present and consuming memory. Widgets can be moved around on the parent window using the `Move()` function. `Move()` moves the center of an image or label to the specified pixel, counting from the upper-left corner of the screen. `Move()` moves the upper left-hand corner of textboxes. For the sake of convenience, the `MoveCorner` function is available, which will move an image or label by its upper left-hand corner.

You should remove widgets from their parent window when you are finished using them.

All widgets have several properties available for controlling their behavior.

```
widget.name
```

```
widget.X
widget.Y
widget.WIDTH
widget.HEIGHT
widget.VISIBLE
widget.ROTATION
widget.ZOOMX
widget.ZOOMY
```

4.6 Images

PEBL can read numerous image types, courtesy of the **SDL_image** library. Use the `MakeImage()` function to read an image into an image object. As images are often used as stimuli, `Move()` centers the image on the specified point. To move by the upper-left hand corner, use the PEBL-defined `MoveCorner()` function:

```
define MoveCorner(object, x, y)
{
  size    <- GetSize(object)
  centerX <- x + First(size)/2
  centerY <- y + Last(size)/2
  Move(object, centerX, centerY)
}
```

Images have all the properties available for widgets, but the width and height can only be read, and not set. Width and height are controlled by the dimensions of the image file.

4.7 Canvases

A canvas is a blank rectangle, sort of like an 'imageless' image. As with an image, `Move()` centers the image on the specified point. A canvas appears similar to a Rectangle() shape, but differs in some important ways. First, a Canvas has a piece of video memory associated with it–shapes do not. This means that other objects can be added to a canvas, just as it can be added to a window. If you move the canvas around, the attached objects will move with the canvas.

Second, individual pixels of a canvas can be set, using the SetPoint() function. SetPoint works on images too, but not on text. This is because a Draw() command re-renders text, and so will wipe out any pixel damage you have done. This can be useful for making special-purpose drawing functions to create stimuli, especially noise distributions.

Finally, a canvas can be drawn on with another object. In fact, you can you another image as a brush. Add an image to a canvas, and anytime you call Draw() on the canvas (rather than without an argument), the image gets imprinted on the canvas. This will remain until you call ResetCanvas().

For example:

```
tb   <- MakeCanvas(600,400,d)
AddObject(tb,win)

##add the image to canvas, not win
pebl <- MakeImage("pebl.png")
AddObject(pebl,tb)

##Nothing will appear on the screen in these intermediate draws
Move(pebl,100,100)
Draw(pebl)
Move(pebl,200,100)
Draw(pebl)
Move(pebl,200,200)
Draw(pebl)
Move(pebl,100,200)
Draw(pebl)

Draw()   ##Now, we will see the canvas with 4 pebl images on it.
```

The draw-on trick can be used to add noise to a text stimulus. Make a label and add it to a canvas, use Draw() on the label, then hide the label, and add noise to the canvas by using SetPoint(). Anything drawn on the canvas won't get reset until the ResetCanvas() function is called.

Images have all the properties available for widgets. Size cannot be updated once the canvas is created.

Note that the background color can have an alpha value. If you use an alpha value of 0, the background will be invisible.

4.8   Shapes

PEBL allows you to define a number of shape objects that can be added to another widget. A demonstration script exercising these shapes is found in demo/shapes.pbl.

The following is a list of shape and their properties.

4.8.1   Circle

Description: A standard circle. Move commands move the center of the circle to the specified location.

Command: Circle(<x>,<y>,<r>,<color>,<filled>)

Properties: .name
.filled = 0,1 (whether it is filled)
.color (color)
.x (x position of center)
.y (y position of center)
.height (read-only height)

.width (read-only width)
.R (radius)

4.8.2 Ellipse

Description: An ellipse, with height and width differing. Cannot be pointed in an arbitrary direction. Move commands move the center of the shape to the specified location.
Command: `Ellipse(<x>,<y>,<rx>,<ry>,<color>,<filled>)`

Properties: .name
.filled = 0,1 (whether it is filled)
.color (color)
.x (x position of center)
.y (y position of center)
.height (read-only height)
.width (read-only width)
.rx (x radius)
.ry (y radius

4.8.3 Square

Description: A square. Move commands move the center of the shape to the specified location.
Command: `Square(<x>,<y>,<size>,<color>,<filled>)`

Properties:
.name
.filled = 0,1 (whether it is filled)
.color (color)
.x (x position of center)
.y (y position of center)
.height (read-only height)
.width (read-only width)
.dx, .dy, .size (Length of side)

4.8.4 Rectangle

Description: A Rectangle. Move commands move the center of the rectangle to the specified location.
Command: `Rectangle(<x>,<y>,<dx>,<dy>,<color>,<filled>)`

Properties: .name
.filled = 0,1 (whether it is filled)

.color (color)
.x (x position of center)
.y (y position of center)
.height (read-only height)
.width (read-only width)
.dx, (width) .dy, (height)

4.8.5   Line

Description: A Line. Move commands move the center of the line to the specified location.
Command: `Line( <x>, <y>,<dx>,<dy>,<color>)`

Properties: .color (color)
.x (x position of start)
.y (y position of start)
.width, (x length)
.height, (y length)

4.8.6   Polygon

Description: An arbitrary polygon.
Command: `Polygon( <x>, <y>,<xpoints>,<ypoints>,<color>,<filled>)`

Properties: .name
.color (color)
.x (x position of start)
.y (y position of start)

4.8.7   Bezier

Description: An arbitrary bezier curve.
Command: `Bezier( <x>, <y>,<xpoints>,<ypoints>,<steps>,<color>)`

Properties: .name
.color (color)
.x (x position of start)
.y (y position of start)

4.9   Text Labels

You can create a text label object with the `MakeLabel()` function, which requires specifying a font, and the foreground and background colors. Labels are only a single line of text. Like images, when you move them, they center on the specified point.

The text inside a label can be extracted with `GetText()` and set with `SetText()`. When you change a text object, it will not appear until the next time you call a `Draw()` function.

Text labels have all the regular widget properties, plus:

```
label.TEXT
label.FONT
```

The `.HEIGHT` and `.WIDTH` accessible, but cannot be changed because they are controlled by the text and the font size.

4.10   Text Boxes

A text box is a graphical widget that contains a body of text. Text automatically wraps when it is too long to fit on a single line. Like labels, the text inside a TextBox can be extracted with `GetText()` and set with `SetText()`. When a text object is changed, it rerenders immediately, but does not appear until the next time a `Draw()` function is called.

Textbox properties:

```
textbox.EDITABLE
textbox.CURSORPOS
```

4.11   User-Editable Text Boxes

Text box editing can be performed using the `GetInput(<textbox>,<escape-key>)` function. This returns the text that is present in the box when the participant hits the key associated with `<escape-key>`. `<escape-key>` is just a text-based code that describes the keypress that should be checked for exit. Typical escape-key options include:

```
"<return>"
"<esc>"
"<backspace>"
"<kp_enter>"
" "
"A"
```

See the Keyboard Entry section below for a more complete list.

Translation from string to keyboard input is still crude, and is handled in `src/utility/PEBLUtility.cpp:TranslateString`

4.12   Audio

Currently, audio output is very primitive, and there are no facilities for recording or analyzing audio input. Audio `.wav` files can be loaded with the `LoadSound()` function, which returns an audio stream object that can be played with either the `PlayForeground()` or `PlayBackground()` functions. The `PlayForeground()` function returns once the sound is finished playing; `PlayBackground()` returns immediately and the sound plays in a separate thread. When using `PlayBackground`, playing can be stopped using the `Stop()` function. If another `PlayForeground()` or `PlayBackground()` is then used, the initial sound will immediately terminate and the new file will play. Currently, PEBL can only play one sound at a time.

4.13   Movie Files

If compiled to support them, PEBL can read numerous video and audio media files **waave** library and ffmpeg. Use the `LoadMovie()` function to read a movie file into a movie object. The `Move()` function moves the upper left corner of the movie to the specified point. An audio file can be similarly loaded using the `LoadAudioFile` function.

Movie playback is done via a handler placed in the event loop. This handler is placed there with the `StartPlayback` function. Then, when the event loop runs, the movie will get updated in proper time sequence. The event loop is used for most WaitFor type events. This allows you to play a movie and wait for a response at the same time. Alternately, a complete movie file can be played in full (with no possibility for stopping early) using the PlayMovie() function.

Movies have a number of properties that can be set to change playback or determine aspects of the movie. These are all accessible via .property syntax, and can be printed by the PrintProperties function. Properties include:

- DURATION: time in ms

- FILENAME: filename

- HEIGHT: pixels high

- NAME: <MOVIE>

- PLAYBACKPOSITION: where playback is

- ROTATION: Inherited; will not work

- VISIBLE: whether hidden or visible

- VOLUME: volume on a logarithmic scale–can go from 0 to +infinity

- WIDTH: screen width in pixels

- X: upper left corner x

- Y: upper left corner y

- ZOOMX: scaling; not used (just set width)

- ZOOMY: scaling; not used (just set height)

4.14   Keyboard Entry

PEBL can examine the state of the keyboard, and wait for various keyboard events to happen. Functions such as `WaitForKeyDown()`, `WaitForAnyKeyDown()`, etc., allow you to collect responses from subjects. Most keys are specified by their letter name; others have special names:
```
"<left>"
"<up>"
"<down>"
"<right>"
"<enter>"
"<return>"
"<esc>"
"<backspace>" or "<back>"
"<kp_0>" through "<kp_9>", as well as "<kp_period>", "<kp_divide>",
 "<kp_multiply>", "<kp_minus>", "<kp_plus>", "<kp_equals>",
"<kp_enter>" for  keypad keys.
```

```
 "<insert>","<delete>", "<home>", "<end>","<pageup>","<pagedown>" for other
special keys.
```

```
Function keys "<F1>" through "<F15>".
```

Also, the traditional "modifier" keys can serve as normal keys:

```
<lshift>, <rshift> <numlock>, <capslock>, <scrollock>,
<rctrl>, <lctrl>, <ralt>,<lalt>,<rmeta>,<lmeta>,<lsuper>,
<rsuper>,<mode>,<compose>
```

4.15   Joystick Input

PEBL supports input with a joystick. In order to use a joystick, you first need to poll the computer to determine whether a joystick is attached, and create a joystick object. The file joysticktest.pbl in the demo directory creates a simple visual depiction of a fairly standard gamepad.

A joystick will have up to four types of inputs on it: buttons, axes, hats, and balls. But different joysticks are different, and so you may need to do some checking and testing for your particular setup. PEBL currently does not support force-feedback or rumble functions available on some joysticks.

Axes:

Each axis takes on a value between 1 and 32768. For a normal hand-grasp joystick , the first two axis will be determined by the relative x and y positions of the joystick. Gamepads often have triggers that are additional axis, or sometimes there are throttles (or gas/brake pedals in driving devices) that are mapped to axes. Find out how many axes exist with `GetNumJoystickAxes()`. Get the state of a particula axis with `GetJoystickAxisState()`.

Hats:

Hats are the little 8-way buttons that control direction on many game pads. They are sort of a digital axis, because each state is absolute. The entire hat state takes on a single integer number between 0 and 15. It is binary coded to specify whether each of the four major axes buttons are depressed:

- left: 8

- bottom: 4

- right: 2

- top: 1

The mechanics of the hat allows two buttons to be pressed simultaneously, indicating, for example, southeast or northwest. An example of how to extract the bitwise button states is found in the joysticktest.pbl file.

Buttons:

Usually, the state of each of the buttons on the joystick can be identified. Button state is coded so that 0=unpressed, 1=pressed. There can easily be a dozen or more buttons on a joystick, enabling some pretty elaborate response modes for experiments.

Balls:

Balls are very rare; you may have seen them in old-style arcade games like Arkenoid. No consumer joysticks available today appear to have balls that operate this way, and they have not been tested in PEBL. If you want to support trackballs, there are plenty of trackball mice that work as normal joystick controllers.

A number of functions are available for creating a joystick object and polling the joystick's current state:

Summary of joystick functions:

```
GetNumJoysticks()
OpenJoystick()
GetNumJoystickAxes()
```

```
GetNumjJoystickBalls()
GetNumJoystickButtons()
GetNumJoystickHats()
GetJoystickAxisState()
GetJoystickHatState()
GetJoystickButtonState()
```

Currently, the joystick state is not integrated into PEBL's event loop. Consequently, there are no functions such as WaitForJoystickButton(), and no way to create or monitor events. To use the joystick, you need to monitor the state of the device manually, and create a polling loop yourself, like:

```
##This will keep looping until you press the first button
js < OpenJoystick(1)  ##open the first joystick connected to the system
gCont <- 1
while (gCont)
  {
    state <- GetJoystickAxisState(js,1)
    Print(state)
    ##Do something with the axis1 here


    gCont <- GetJoystickButtonState(1)
  }
```

The file demo/joysticktest.pbl uses most of the available joystick functions to display a virtual gamepad on the screen as it captures input.

4.16 Files

Files are objects that can be read from or written to using several PEBL functions. To use a file object, create one using one of the functions listed below. Each function returns a file object:
```
FileOpenRead()
FileOpenWrite()
FileOpenAppend()
```

For example, you can use the command:
`myfile <- FileOpenRead("stimuli.txt")`
to create 'myfile', a readable file stream.
Other Functions described below allow filestreams to be written to or read from. When you are finished, you can close a filestream Using the 'FileClose()' function.

4.17 Network Connections

PEBL has limited ability to open and communicate via TCP/IP connections, either some other system (e.g., for synchronizing with an e.e.g. or eyetracking computer), or another computer running PEBL (e.g., to create multi-subject game theory experiments or to have an experimenter controlling the task from another computer.)

4.17.1   TCP/IP Overview

TCP/IP is a protocol by which computers can talk to one another. It is fairly barebones, and PEBL tries to hide much of its complexity. The information you send from one computer to another is guaranteed to arrive in the correct order, at the potential cost of serious delays, especially if the computers are on different networks or in different locations. Furthermore, connecting PEBL to another computer in this way is a potential security risk. However, the ability to transfer information between computers opens up huge potential for the types of experiments that can be constructed.

4.17.2   Addresses and Ports

To do this, you first must open a network object to communicate with another computer. To do this, you must know (1) the IP number (like 127.0.0.1) or hostname (like myname.myschool.edu) of the computer you want to connect to, and (2) the port you want to connect on. You can even use the protocol to connect to another program running on your own computer, by specifying an IP address of 127.0.0.1, or the hostname "localhost". A port is a number–usually 2 to 5 digits, specifying a type of service on your computer. Many ports are frequently used for specific types of communication, but you can use any port you wish to communicate, as long as both computers know this port. Most ports on your computer should be blocked by default, so you may need to turn off your firewall or allow your chosen port to pass through the security or you may have trouble communicating.

To allow two PEBL programs to communicate, you need to decide that one computer is the "server" and the other is the "client". On the server, you execute the function `WaitForNetworkConnection(port)`, which listens on the specified port until the client tries to connect. After the server is started, the client calls `ConnectToHost(hostname, port)` or `AcceptNetworkConnection(port)` `ConnectToIP(ipnum, port)`, depending upon whether you are using the hostname or ip address. Typically, ip numbers are specified by four three-digit numbers separated by dots, like 196.168.0.1. This actually represents a 4-byte integer, and this 4-byte integer is what `ConnectToIP()` expects. To create that integer, use the function
`ConvertIPString(ipnum)`, which accepts an IP address specified in a string. So, you can use:
`net <- ConnectToIP(ConvertIPString( "127.0.0.1"), 1234)`
to create a connection to another program listening on port 1234 on your own computer. These functions all return a network object (e.g., **net**) that must be used in later communication.

4.17.3 Sending and Receiving Data

Once connected, the distinction between client and server essentially disappears. However, to communicate, one computer must send data with the `SendData(net, data)`, and the other must receive the data, using the `GetData(net, size)` function. PEBL can only send text strings, and you must know the length of the message you want to receive. More complex communication can be done by creating a set of PEBL functions that encapsulate messages into text strings with templated headers that specify the message length. Then, to receive a message, you first read the fixed-length header, determine how much more data needs to be read, then read in the rest of the data.

4.17.4 Closing networks

If you are using a network connection to synchronize timing of two computers, you probably want to close the network connection with `CloseNetworkConnection(net)` after you have synchronized, to avoid any extra overhead.

A simple example of an experiment that uses TCP/IP to communicate is the NIM game in demo/nim.pbl.

4.18 Parallel Port

Starting with Version 0.12, PEBL can send and receive information via a standard parallel (printer) port. These don't appear on many computers anymore, but you can still get them, and they are still important ways to interface with hardware devices such as EEG and MRI machines and homebrew button boxes. Currently, parallel port access is fairly limited to setting and getting the state of the 8 data bits. Parallel ports have a number of bits you can play with, but currently PEBL only supports the basic 8 data bits. Basically, you can set the state of the bits or read the state of the bits, which can either control things like LEDs, or be impacted by making connections between the ground and the data bit.

If you have a parallel port, it is mapped to one of three ports: LPT1, LPT2, or LPTX. To initialize access to a port, you must call OpenPPort with the name of your port:

```
port <- OpenPPort("LPT1")
```

Parallel ports have two modes, input and output. To read data in, it needs to be in input mode; to change the state of the bits, it needs to be in output mode. Set the state with SetPPortMode(port,"¡input¿") or SetPPortMode(port,"¡output¿").

To access the state of a port, use GetPPortState(port). It will return a string of "—" separated 1s and 0s, which specify the state of each of the 8 bits.

To set the state of the port, use SetPPortState(port,state). state should be a list of 8 0s or 1s:

SetPPortState(port, [0,0,0,0,0,0,0,1])

The internal c++ parallel port classes have substantially more flexibility, and can be adapted to do more complex access of parallel ports.

4.19   Serial Port

- OPENCOMPORT
- COMPORTSENDBYTE
- COMPORTGETBYTE

4.20   The Event Loop

To assist in testing for multiple input events simultaneously, PEBL implements an event loop that will quickly scan multiple conditions and execute proper results whenever any one condition is met.

The event loop works by maintaining a list of triggers that can be satisfied by various conditions. The conditions typically specify a device or other data source to examine, such as the timer. On each cycle of the loop, all events are examined, and when any of them are satisfied, either a specified function will be executed, or the event loop will exit. Most of the timing and input functions use the event loop behind the scenes.

As of Version 0.12, simple means to program the event loop are available. Three functions include:

- RegisterEvent(). This allows you to specify a condition and a function name which executes whenever the condition is true.

- StartEventLoop(). This starts the event loop, with all available events.

- ClearEventLoop(). This clears out the event loop so other events can be used.

Note that because other functions, such as Wait(), use the event loop, you can pre-load extra events and start the event loop with one of these functions.

These are used in a number of test battery tasks. However, their use is currently somewhat experimental, and their names and arguments may change in the future, and so we will not provide a detailed description of their use here.

4.21   Errors and Warnings

PEBL does a great deal of error-checking to ensure that your program will run. If you crash with a segmentation fault, this is an error and you should report it. When a fatal error or non-fatal warning occurs, PEBL attempts to identify the location in your input file that led to the warning. On Linux, the warning and this location are printed to the command-line upon exit; on MS Windows or if you are using the launcher on any platform, they are printed to the file `stderr.txt`.

You can do error checking in your own scripts with the `SignalFatalError()` function. This is especially useful in combination with the functions testing the type of object passed into the function. To ensure proper processing and ease of debugging, test the format of an argument passed into a function:

```
define MyFunction(par)
 {
  if(not IsList(par))
  {
   SignalFatalError("MyFunction passed a non-list variable.")
  }
  ##Do other stuff here
 }
```

4.22   Paths and Path Searching

Numerous functions and objects open files on your computer to read in information such as graphics, sounds, fonts, program files, and text files. When you attempt to open a file, PEBL will search in a number of places, in this order:

- The (current) working directory

- The directory of each file specified in the command line arguments

- media/fonts

- media/sounds

- media/images

- media/text

You can also specify other paths to be searched by specifying them on the command line. Be sure to end the directory with whatever is appropriate for your platform, e.g. '\' on Microsoft Windows or '/' on Linux.
On OSX, as of version 0.12, the media/ directory is located within the Resources/ subdirectory of the application package.

4.23   Provided Media Files

PEBL comes with various media files that can be specified from any script without including the complete path. If a user's file has the same name, it will be loaded before the PEBL-provided version. Table 4.2 describes the files included.

Table 4.2: Media Files Provided with PEBL

Name	Description
In 'media/fonts/':	
Listing of fonts appears in Table 4.1	
In 'media/images/':	
pebl.bmp	Demonstration bitmap image
pebl.png	Demonstration PNG image
smiley-small.png	25x25 smiley face
frowney-small.png	25x25 frowney face
smiley-large.png	100x100 smiley face
frowney-large.png	100x100 frowney face
plus.png	A green plus sign
x.png	A red x sign, matching the red plus
In 'media/sounds/':	
buzz500ms.wav	A 500-ms buzzer
chirp1.wav	A chirp stimulus
boo.wav	A really bad booing sound
cheer.wav	A pretty lame cheering sound
beep.wav	A simple beep
In 'media/text/':	
Consonants.txt	List of all consonants, both cases
Digits.txt	List of digits 0-9
DigitNames.txt	List of digit names
Letters.txt	All letters, both cases
Lowercase.txt	Lowercase letters
LowercaseConsonants.txt	Lowercase Consonants
LowercaseVowels.txt	Lowercase Vowels
Uppercase.txt	Uppercase Letters
UppercaseConsonants.txt	Uppercase Consonants
UppercaseVowels.txt	Uppercase Vowels
Vowels.txt	Vowels (both cases)

Additionally, the PEBL Project distributes a number of other media files separately from the base system. These are available for separate download on the pebl website (http://pebl.sourceforge.net), and include a set of images (including shapes and sorting-task cards), and a set of auditory recordings (including beeps, the digits 0-10, and a few other things).

4.24 Special Variables

There are a number of special variables that be set by PEBL, and can later be accessed by an experiment. These are described in table 4.3.

Table 4.3: Special Variables in PEBL

Name	Purpose
gKeepLooping	Controls continued execution in event loop (unused).
gSleepEasy	Sets 'busy-waiting' to be either on or off. Busy-waiting can improve timing, but is often not needed and pegs CPU.
gVideoWidth	The width in pixels of the display (set by default or command-line option). Changing this before calling `MakeWindow` will change display width, if that width is available.
gVideoHeight	The height in pixels of the display (set by default or command-line). Change this before using `MakeWindow()` to change the display height
gVideoDepth	The bit depth of the video.
gSubNum	A global variable set to whatever follows the `--s` or `--S` command-line argument. Defaults to "0".
gLanguage	A global variable specified on the command line which can be used by a script to target a specific language. Defaults to 'en'.
gQuote	A quotation mark: ". Use it to add quotes in text.
gClick	[x,y] location last click in WaitForClickOnTarget.
gPEBLBaseFont	Name of the default font to use in helper functions and most battery tasks. By default, set to "DejaVuSans.ttf". Change to override.
gPEBLBaseFontMono	Name of the default mono-spaced font By default, it is set to "DejaVuSansMono.ttf".
gPEBLBaseFontSerif	Name of the default serif font. By default, it is set to "DejaVuSerif.ttf".

Chapter 5

Function Quick Reference

Table 5.1 lists the functions available for use with PEBL. Those that are unimplemented are noted as such. If you want the functionality of an unimplemented function, or want functionality not provided in any of these functions, contact us, or better yet, contribute to the PEBL project by implementing the function yourself.

Table 5.1: Function Quick Reference

Name	Arguments	Description
\multicolumn{3}{Math Functions}		
Log10	\<num\>	Log base 10 of \<num\>
Log2	\<num\>	Log base 2 of \<num\>
Ln	\<num\>	Natural log of \<num\>
LogN	\<num\> \<base\>	Log base \<base\> of \<num\>
Exp	\<pow\>	e to the power of \<pow\>
Pow	\<num\> \<pow\>	\<num\> to the power of \<pow\>
Sqrt	\<num\>	Square root of \<num\>
NthRoot	\<num\> \<root\>	\<num\> to the power of 1/\<root\>
Tan	\<deg\>	Tangent of \<deg\> degrees
Sin	\<deg\>	Sine of \<deg\> degrees
Cos	\<deg\>	Cosine of \<deg\> degrees
ATan	\<num\>	Inverse Tan of \<num\>, in degrees
ASin	\<num\>	Inverse Sine of \<num\>, in degrees
ACos	\<num\>	Inverse Cosine of \<num\>, in degrees
DegToRad	\<deg\>	Converts degrees to radians
RadToDeg	\<rad\>	Converts radians to degrees
Round	\<num\>, (optional) \<precision\>	Rounds \<num\> to nearest integer, or optionally power of 1/ten precision.
Floor	\<num\>	Rounds \<num\> down to the next integer
Ceiling	\<num\>	Rounds \<num\> up to the next integer

Name	Arguments	Description
AbsFloor	\<num\>	Rounds \<num\> toward 0 to an integer
Mod	\<num\> \<mod\>	Returns \<num\> mod \<mod\> or remainder of \<num\>/\<mod\>
Div	\<num\> \<mod\>	Returns round(\<num\>/\<mod\>)
ToInteger	\<num\>	Rounds a number to an integer, and changes internal representation
ToFloat	\<num\>	Converts number to internal floating-point representation
ToNumber	\<\>	
ToString	\<num\>	Converts a numerical value to a string representation
Sign	\<num\>	Returns +1 or -1, depending on sign of argument
Abs	\<num\>	Returns the absolute value of the number
CumNormInv	\<p\>	Returns accurate numerical approximation of cumulative normal inverse.
NormalDensity	\<x\>	Returns density of standard normal distribution.
SDTDPrime	\<hr\>,\<far\>	Computes SDT dprime.
SDTBeta	\<hr\>,\<far\>	Computes SDT beta.
Order	\<list\>	Returns a list of integers representing the order of \<list\>
Rank	\<list\>	Returns integers representing the ranked indices of the numbers of\<list\>
Median	\<list\>	Returns the median value of the numbers in \<list\>
Min	\<list\>	Returns the smallest of \<list\>
Max	\<list\>	Returns the largest of \<list\>
StDev	\<list\>	Returns the standard dev of \<list\>
Sum	\<list\>	Returns the sum of the numbers in \<list\>
Median	\<list\>	Returns the median of a set of values
Quantile	\<list\> \<num\>	Returns the \<num\> quantile of the numbers in \<list\>
SummaryStats	\<data\>,\<cond\>	Returns statistics (cond, N, median, mean, sd) computed on data for each distinct value of \<cond\>
SeedRNG	\<num\>	Seeds the random number generator with \<num\> to reproduce a random sequence
RandomizeTimer	-	Seeds the RNG with the current time

Name	Arguments	Description
Random	-	Returns a random number between 0 and 1
RandomDiscrete	<num>	Returns a random integer between 1 and <num>
RandomUniform	<num>	Returns a random floating-point number between 0 and <num>
RandomNormal	<mean> <stdev>	Returns a random number according to the standard normal distribution with <mean> and <stdev>
RandomExponential	<mean>	Returns a random number according to exponential distribution with mean <mean> (or decay 1/mean)
RandomLogistic	<p>	Returns a random number according to the logistic distribution with parameter <p>
RandomLogNormal	<median> <spread>	Returns a random number according to the log-normal distribution with parameters <median> and <spread>
RandomBinomial	<p> <n>	Returns a random number according to the Binomial distribution with probability <p> and repetitions <n>
RandomBernoulli	<p>	Returns 0 with probability (1-<p>) and 1 with probability <p>
ZoomPoints	<[xs,yy]>, <xzoom>, <yzoom>	Zooms a set of points in 2 directions
ReflectPoints	<[xs,yy]>	Reflects points on vertical axis
RotatePoints	<[xs,yy]>,<angle>	Rotates point <angle> degrees
GetAngle	<x>,<y>	Returns the angle in degrees of a vector.
Dist	<x1,y1>,<[x2,y2]>	Returns distance between two points.
ToRight	<p1,p2,p3>	Determines whether p3 is te the right of line p1p2
GetAngle3	<a,b,c>	Gets angle abc.
SegmentsIntersect	<ax,ay,bx,by,cx,cy,dx,dy>	Determines whether line segment ax intersects cd.
NonOverlapLayout	<xmin,xmax,ymin,ymax,tol,num>	Creates a set of num points that don't overlap, but fails gracefully
LayoutGrid	<minx,maxx,miny,maxy,height,width,vertical>	Creates [x,y] pairs in a grid for graphical layout

Name	Arguments	Description
	File/Network/Device Functions	
`Print`	`<value>`	Prints `<value>` to `stdout`, appending a new line afterwards. `stdout` is the console (in Linux) or the file `stdout.txt` (in Windows)
`Print_`	`<value>`	Prints `<value>` to stdout, without appending a newline afterwards
`PrintList`	`<value>`	Prints `<list>`, getting rid of '[', ']' and ',' characters.
`Format`	`<object> <size>`	Prints a number with specified spaces by truncating or padding
`ZeroPad`	`<number> <size>`	Pads the beginning of a number with 0s so the number is size long
`FileOpenRead`	`<filename>`	Opens a filename, returning a stream to be used for reading information
`FileOpenWrite`	`<filename>`	Opens a filename, returning a stream that can be used for writing information. Creates new file if file already exists
`FileOpenOverwrite`	`<filename>`	Opens a filename, returning a stream that can be used for writing information. Overwrites if file already exists
`FileOpenAppend`	`<filename>`	Opens a filename, returning a stream that can be used for writing info. Appends if the file already exists, opens if file does not
`FileClose`	`<filestream>`	Closes a filestream variable. Pass the variable name, not the filename
`FilePrint`	`<filestream>` `<value>`	Like `Print`, but to a file.
`FilePrint_`	`<filestream>` `<value>`	Like `Print_`, but to a file.
`FilePrintList`	`<file><list>`	Prints `<list>` to `<file>`, getting rid of '[', ']' and ',' characters.
`FileReadCharacter`	`<filestream>`	Reads and returns a single character from a filestream
`FileReadWord`	`<filestream>`	Reads and returns a 'word' from a file; the next connected stream of characters not including a ' ' or a newline. Will not read newline characters

44

Name	Arguments	Description
`FileReadLine`	`<filestream>`	Reads and returns a line from a file; all characters up until the next newline or the end of the file
`FileReadList`	`<filename>`	Given a filename, will open it, read in all the items into a list (one item per line), and close the file afterwards
`FileReadTable`	`<filename>` `<opt-sep>`	Like `FileReadList`, but reads in tables. Optionally, specify a token separator
`ReadCSV`	`<filename>`	Opens a csv file¡ returning a table with its elements
`FileReadText`	`<filename>`	Reads all of the text in the file into a variable
`EndOfLine`	`<filestream>`	Returns true if at end of line
`EndOfFile`	`<filestream>`	Returns true if at the end of a file
`GetDirectoryListing`	`<path>`	Returns a list of all the files/subdirectories in a path
`FileExists`	`<path>`	Checks whether a file exists
`IsDirectory`	`<path>`	Checks whether a file is a directory
`MakeDirectory`	`<path>,<dirname>`	Creates a directory in path
`RemoveFile`	`<file>`	Removes and deletes a file
`AppendFile`	`<file1> ,<file2>`	Appends a file2 to file1
`DeleteFile`	`<file1>`	Deletes a file
`ConnectToIP`	`<ip> <port>`	Connects to a port on another computer, returning network object.
`ConnectToHost`	`<hostname>` `<port>`	Connects to a port on another computer, returning network object.
`WaitForNetworkConnection`	`<port>`	Listens on a port until another computer connects, returning a network object
`CloseNetworkConnection`	`<network>`	Closes network connection
`SendData`	`<network>` `<datastring>`	Sends a data string over connection.
`GetData`	`<network>` `<length>`	return a string from network connection
`ConvertIPString`	`<ip-as-string>`	Converts an ip-number-as-string to usable address
`OpenNetworkListener`	`<port>`	Opens a port for listening
`CheckForNetworkConnection`	`<network>`	Checks for incoming connection
`WritePNG`	`<filename>, <object>`	Makes a .png from a window or object

Name	Arguments	Description
GetNumJoysticks	no argument	Determines how many joysticks are available
OpenJoystick	joystick_id	Gets a joystick object
GetNumJoystickAxes	joystick_object	Counts how many axes on a joystick
GetNumJoystickBalls	joystick_object	Counts how many balls on a joystick
GetNumJoystickButtons	joystick_object	Counts how many buttons on a joystick
GetNumJoystickHats	joystick_object	Counts how many hats on a joystick
GetJoystickAxisState	joystick_object, axis_id	Gets the state of a joystick axis
GetJoystickHatState	joystick_object, hat_id	Gets the state of a joystick hat
GetJoystickButtonState	joystick_object, button_id	Gets the state of a joystick button
GetJoystickBallState	joystick_object, ball_id	Gets the state of a joystick ball
OpenCOMPort	<portnum>, <baud>	Opens a serial (com) port
COMPortGetByte	<port>	Gets a byte from the comport
COMPortSendByte	<port>,<byte>	Sends a character to the comport
OpenPPort	<portname>	Opens parallel port
SetPPortMode	<port> <mode>	Sets parallel port mode (input/output)
SetPPortState	<port> <state>	Sets parallel port state
GetPPortState	<port>	Gets state of parallel port data bits

Graphical Objects Functions

Name	Arguments	Description
MakeWindow	<colorname>	Creates main window, in color named by argument, or grey if no argument is named
MakeImage	<filename>	Creates an image by reading in an image file (jpg, gif, png, bmp, etc.)
MakeLabel	<text> <font>	Creates a single line of text filled with <text> written in font <font>
MakeTextBox	<text> <font> <width> <height>	Creates a sized box filled with <text> written in font <font>
MakeCanvas	<width>, <height>, <color>	Creates a blank canvas to add objects to or draw on

Name	Arguments	Description
ResetCanvas	`<canvas>`	Resets a canvas to its background, erasing anything drawn on the canvas
EasyLabel	`<text>` `<x><y>` `<win><fontsize>`	Creates a single line of text and adds it to win at `<x><y>`
EasyTextBox	`<text>` `<x>` `<y>` `<win>` `<fontsize>` `<width>` `<height>`	Creates a textbox and adds it to `<win>` at `<x><y>`
MakeColor	`<colorname>`	Creates a color based on a color name
MakeColorRGB	`<red>` `<green>` `<blue>`	Creates a color based on red, green, and blue values
RGBToHSV	`<color>`	Converts a color to HSV triple
MakeFont	`<ttf_filename>` `<style>` `<size>` `<fgcolor>` `<bgcolor>` `<anti-aliased>`	Creates a font which can be used to make labels
SetCursorPosition	`<textbox>` `<position>`	Move the editing cursor in a textbox
GetCursorPosition	`<textbox>`	Gets the position of the editing cursor
SetEditable	`<textbox>` `<status>`	Turns on or off the editing cursor
GetTextBoxCursorFromClick	`<relx>,<rely>`	Gets a cursor position (in characters) from a mouse click.
GetText	`<textobject>`	Returns the text in a textbox or label
GetInput	`<textbox>` `<escape-key>`	Allows a textbox to be edited by user, returning its text when `<escape-key>` is pressed.
SetText	`<textobject>,` `<text>`	Sets the text in a textbox or label
SetFont	`<textobject>,` `<font>`	Changes the font of a text object
Move	`<object> <x> <y>`	Move an object (e.g., an image or a label to an x,y location)
MoveCorner	`<object> <x> <y>`	Moves an image or label by its upper corner.
GetSize	`<object>`	Returns a list of dimensions `<x,y>` of a graphical object.
AddObject	`<object>` `<parent>`	Adds an object to a parent object (window)

Name	Arguments	Description
RemoveObject	`<object>` `<parent>`	Removes an object from a parent window
Show	`<object>`	Shows an object
Hide	`<object>`	Hides an object
ShowCursor	`<object>`	Hides or show mouse cursor.
GetMouseCursorPosition		Gets [x,y] position of mouse
GetMouseState		Gets [x,y,b1,b2,b3] list of mouse state, including button states
SetMouseCursorPosition	`<x>`,`<y>`	Sets x,y position of mouse
Draw	`<object>` or no argument	Redraws a widget and its children
DrawFor	`<object>` `<cycles>`	Draws for exactly `<cycles>` cycles, then returns
Circle	`<x>` `<y>` `<r>` `<color>` `<filled>`	Creates circle with radius r centered at position x,y
Ellipse	`<x>` `<y>` `<rx>` `<ry>``<color>` `<filled>`	Creates ellipse with radii rx and ry centered at position x,y
Square	`<x>` `<y>` `<size>` `<color>` `<filled>`	Creates square with width size centered at position x,y
Rectangle	`<x>` `<y>` `<dx>` `<dy>``<color>` `<filled>`	Creates rectangle with size (dx, dy) centered at position x,y
Line	`<x>` `<y>` `<dx>` `<dy>` `<color>`	Creates line starting at x,y and ending at x+dx, y+dy
PrintProperties	`<object>`	Prints a list of all available properties of an object (for debugging)
Polygon	`<x>` `<y>` `<xpoints>` `<ypounts>` `<color>``<filled>`	Creates polygon centered at x,y with relative points `<xpoints>`,`<ypoints>`
Bezier	`<x>` `<y>` `<xpoints>` `<ypounts>` `<steps>` `<color>`	Creates bezier curve centered at x,y with relative points `<xpoints>`,`<ypoints>`
BlockE	`<x>` `<y>` `<h>` `<w>` `<thickness>` `<orientation>` `<color>`	Creates a block E as a useable polygon which can be added to a window directly.
Plus	`<x>` `<y>` `<size>` `<w>` `<color>`	Creates a plus sign as a useable polygon which can be added to a window directly.

Name	Arguments	Description
MakeStarPoints	<r_outer> <r_inner> <npeaks>	Creates points for a star, which can then be fed to Polygon
MakeNGonPoints	<radius> <npeaks>	Creates points for a polygon, which can then be fed to Polygon
ThickLine	<x1> <y1> <x2> <y2> <thickness> <color>	Creates a thick line between two points
MakeAttneave	<radius>,numpoints,minangle,maxangle	Makes a complex "Attneave" polygon
ConvexHull	<list-of-pts>Returns a convex subset of points for a set	
KaneszaSquare	squaresize, circleradius,fg,bg	Creates a 'Kanesza Square' stimulus.
KaneszaPolygon	points,circTF, circleradius,fg,bg,show	Create generic Kanesza polygon.
Inside	<[x,y]> <object>	Determines whether a point is inside a graphical object
SetPixel	x,y,color	Sets the color of a pixel on an image or canvas to color
SetPoint	x,y,color	Sets the color of a pixel on an image or canvas to color
GetPixelColor	<obj>,x,y	Gets the color of a specified pixel on a widget
MakeGabor	size,freq,sd, angle,phase,bglev	Creates a 'gabor patch' with specified parameters

Sound Objects Functions

Name	Arguments	Description
LoadSound	<filename>	Loads a soundfile from the filename, returning a variable that can be played
PlayForeground	<sound>	Plays the sound 'in the foreground', not returning until the sound is complete
PlayBackground	<sound>	Plays the sound 'in the background', returning immediately
Stop	<sound>	Stops a sound playing in the background from playing
MakeSineWave	freq,duration,amplitude	Creates a pure sine wave.
MakeAudioInputBuffer	<time-in-ms>	Creates a buffer to record audio input
SaveAudioToWaveFile		

Name	Arguments	Description
	`<filename>,<buffer>`	Saves buffer to a .wav file format
`GetVocalResponseTime`		A simple voice key
	`<buffer>,<threshold>,<duration>`	
`LoadMovie`	`<movie_filename>`	Load a movie file
	`<window>,<width>,<height>`	
`LoadAudioFile`	`<audio_filename>`	Load an audio file
`PlayMovie`	`<movie>`	Plays a movie until its end
`StartPlayback`	`<movie>`	Initiates playback in background, updated with Wait()
`PausePlayback`	`<movie>`	Pauses playback of movie

Misc Event Functions

Name	Arguments	Description
`GetTime`	`<>`	Gets a number, in milliseconds, representing the time since the PEBL program began running.
`Wait`	`<time>`	Pauses execution for `<time>` ms
`IsKeyDown`	`<keyval>`	Determines whether the key associated with `<keyval>` is down
`IsKeyUp`	`<keyval>`	Determines whether the key associated with `<keyval>` is up
`IsAnyKeyDown`	`<>`	Determines whether any key is down.
`WaitForKeyDown`	`<keyval>`	Waits until `<keyval>` is detected to be in the down state
`WaitForAnyKeyDown`	`<>`	Waits until any key is detected in down state
`WaitForKeyUp`	`<keyval>`	Waits until `<keyval>` is in up state.
`WaitForAllKeysUp`		Waits until all keys are in up state
`WaitForAnyKeyDownWithTimeout`		
	`<time>`	Waits for a key to be pressed, but only for `<time>` ms
`WaitForKeyListDown`		
	`<list-of-keyvals>`	Waits until one of the keys is in down state
`WaitForKeyPress`	`<key>`	Waits until `<key>` is pressed
`WaitForAnyKeyPress`	`<>`	Waits until any key is pressed
`WaitForKeyRelease`	`<key>`	Waits until `<key>` is released
`WaitForListKeyPress`		Waits until one of `<list-of-keys>` is
	`<list-of-keys>`	pressed
`WaitForListKeyPressWithTimeout`		
	`<list-of-keyvals>` `<timeout> <type>`	Waits for either a key to be pressed or a time to pass.

Name	Arguments	Description
WaitForMouseButton		Waits until any of the mouse buttons is pressed or released, and returns message indicating what happened
WaitForMouseClickWithTimeout	<timeout>	Waits until any of the mouse buttons is pressed, or a prespecified timout has elapsed.
WaitForClickOnTarget	<target>	Waits until any of a set of target objects are clicked.
WaitForClickOnTargetWithTimeout	<target>, <timeout>	Waits with a max time for a set of targets to be clicked.
WaitForDownClick		Waits for mouse button to be clicked
RegisterEvent	<>	Registers events to trigger based on particular conditions
StartEventLoop	<>	Starts the event loop
ClearEventLoop	<>	Clears all trigger events from event loop
SignalFatalError	<message>	Halts execution, printing out message
TranslateKeyCode	<>	Converts a keycode to a key name
TimeStamp		Returns a string containing the current date and time
GetPEBLVersion	<>	Returns a string indicating which version of PEBL you are using
GetSystemType	<>	Identifies the type of operating system being used.
GetVideoModes	<>	Gets list of available screen resolutions
GetCurrentScreenResolution	<>	Gets the current widthxheight of the screen
SystemCall	<command> <optional-args>	Executes command in operating system
LaunchFile	<file>	Launches a file using platform-specific handlers
GetNIMHDemographics	<code> <window> <file>	Asks NIMH-related questions
GetSubNum	<window>	Asks user to enter subject number
MessageBox	<text> <win>	Pops up a message, overtop the entire screen, and waits for a click to continue.
GetEasyInput	<text> <win>	Gets typed input based on a prompt.
GetEasyChoice	<text>, <choices>,	Simple multiple choice

Name	Arguments	Description
	`<output>`, `<window>`	
CountDown	`<window>`	Displays a 3 2 1 countdown on screen
IsAudioOut	`<variant>`	Tests whether `<variant>` is a AudioOut stream
IsCanvas	`<variant>`	Tests whether `<variant>` is a Canvas
IsColor	`<variant>`	Tests whether `<variant>` is a Color
IsFileStream	`<variant>`	Tests whether `<variant>` is a FileStream
IsFloat	`<variant>`	Tests whether `<variant>` is a floating-point number
IsFont	`<variant>`	Tests whether `<variant>` is a Font
IsImage	`<variant>`	Tests whether `<variant>` is an Image
IsInteger	`<variant>`	Tests whether `<variant>` is an integer-type number
IsLabel	`<variant>`	Tests whether `<variant>` is a Text Label
IsList	`<variant>`	Tests whether `<variant>` is a List
IsNumber	`<variant>`	Tests whether `<variant>` is a number
IsTextBox	`<variant>`	Tests whether `<variant>`is a TextBox
IsText	`<variant>`	Tests whether `<variant>` is a text string
IsShape	`<variant>`	Tests whether `<variant>` is any drawing shape, such as a circle, square or polygon
IsString	`<variant>`	Tests whether `<variant>` is a string
IsWidget	`<variant>`	Tests whether `<variant>` is any Widget
IsWindow	`<variant>`	Tests whether `<variant>` is any Window

List Manipulation Functions

Name	Arguments	Description
Shuffle	`<list>`	Returns a new list with the items in list shuffled randomly.
ShuffleRepeat	`<list> <times>`	Generates a list of n shuffled versions of `<list>`
ShuffleWithoutAdjacents	`<nested-list>`	Shuffle specifying items that should not appear adjacently
Repeat	`<item> <n>`	Repeats an item n times in a list
RepeatList	`<list> <n>`	Makes a new list containing the elements of `<list>` repeated `<n>` times

Name	Arguments	Description
Sequence	`<start>` `<end>` `<step>`	Makes a sequence of numbers from `<start>` to `<end>`, with `<step>`-sized increments
ChooseN	`<list>` `<n>`	Returns a sublist of `<n>` items from a list, in the order they appear in the original list
Sample	`<list>`	Picks a single item randomly from `<list>`.
SampleN	`<list>` `<n>`	Returns a randomly-ordered sublist of `<n>` items from a list
SampleNWithReplacement	`<list>` `<n>`	Returns a sublist of `<n>` items from a list
DesignLatinSquare	`<list1>` `<list2>`	
LatinSquare	`<list>`	A simple latin square constructor
DesignGrecoLatinSquare	`<list1>` `<list2>` `<list3>`	
DesignBalancedSampling	`<list>` `<number>`	
DesignFullCounterbalance	`<list1>` `<list2>`	
CrossFactorWithoutDuplicates	`<list>`	Returns a list of all pairs of items in the list, excluding pairs that where an element appears twice.
Rotate	`<list>` `<n>`	Rotates a list by `<n>` items.
FoldList	`<list>` `<n>`	Folds list into length-n sublists.
Flatten	`<list>`	Flattens a nested list completely
FlattenN	`<list>` `<n>`	Flattens n levels of a nested list
Length	`<list>`	Returns the number of elements in a list.
First	`<list>`	Returns the first item in a list.
Last	`<list>`	Returns the last item in a list.
Merge	`<list1>` `<list2>`	Combines two lists.
Append	`<list>` `<item>`	Returns new list combining `<list>` and `<item>`
PushOnEnd	`<list>` `<item>`	Adds `<item>` to `<list>` efficiently
List	`<item1>` `<item2>`...	Makes a list out of items
Sort	`<list>`	Sorts a list by its values.
SortBy	`<list>` `<key>`	Sorts list by the values in `<key>`
Nth	`<list>` `<n>`	Returns the nth item in a list.
Subset	`<list>` `<list-of-indices>`	returns a subset of items from a list
SetElement	`<list>`, `<index>`, `<value>`	Sets an element of list to value

Name	Arguments	Description
Match	[list],<item>	Returns a list of 0/1s, indicating which elements of list match item.
Filter	[list],<indicators>	Filters a list based on a 0/1 list produced by Match.
Levels	[list]	Returns a sorted list of unique elements in list.
Rest	<list>	Returns a list minus its first element
ExtractListItems	<list> <list-of-indices>	
IsMember	<item> <list>	Checks whether <item> is a member of <list>
Replace	<template> <replacementList>	Replaces items in a data structure
Lookup	<key> <keylist> <database>	returns element in <database> corresponding to element of <keylist> that matches <key>.
Transpose	<list-of-lists>	Transposes a list of equal-length lists.
SubList	<list> <start> <finish>	Returns a sublist of a list.
RemoveSubset	<list> <list-of-pos>	Removes items at positions <list-of-pos> from a list.
ListToString	<list>	Concatenates all elements of a list into a single string
Insert	<list>,<item>,<pos>	Inserts <item> into <list> at <pos>
ListBy	<list>,<conds>	Segments a list into sublist by the values of a second list

String Management Functions		
CR	<num>	Returns string with <num> linefeeds.
Tab	<num>	Returns string with <num> tabs.
Format	<value> <num>	Makes string from value exactly <num> characters by truncating or padding.
Enquote	<text>	Returns string surrounded by quote marks.
Uppercase	<string>	Returns uppercased string
Lowercase	<string>	Returns lowercased string
ReplaceChar	<string> <char> <char2>	Substitutes <char2> for <char> in <string>.

54

Name	Arguments	Description
SplitString	`<string> <split>`	Splits `<string>` into a list of `<split>`-delimited substrings
StringLength	`<string>`	Returns the length of a string
SubString	`<string>` `<position>` `<length>`	Returns a substring
FindInString	`<string> <key>`	Returns position of `<key>` in `<string>`
StripSpace	`<string>`	Strips whitespace from the start and end of `<string>`.
StripQuotes	`<string>`	Strips quotation marks from the start and end of `<string>`.

Chapter 6

The PEBL Launcher

The PEBL Launcher is the best way to navigate and launch PEBL experiments, especially for novices or research assistants. It allows one to specify a few specific options that are frequently changed, navigate through the PEBL Test Battery, and create and save 'experiment chains' to let you run multiple experiments in a row.

Figure 6.1: Screenshot of of PEBL Launcher.

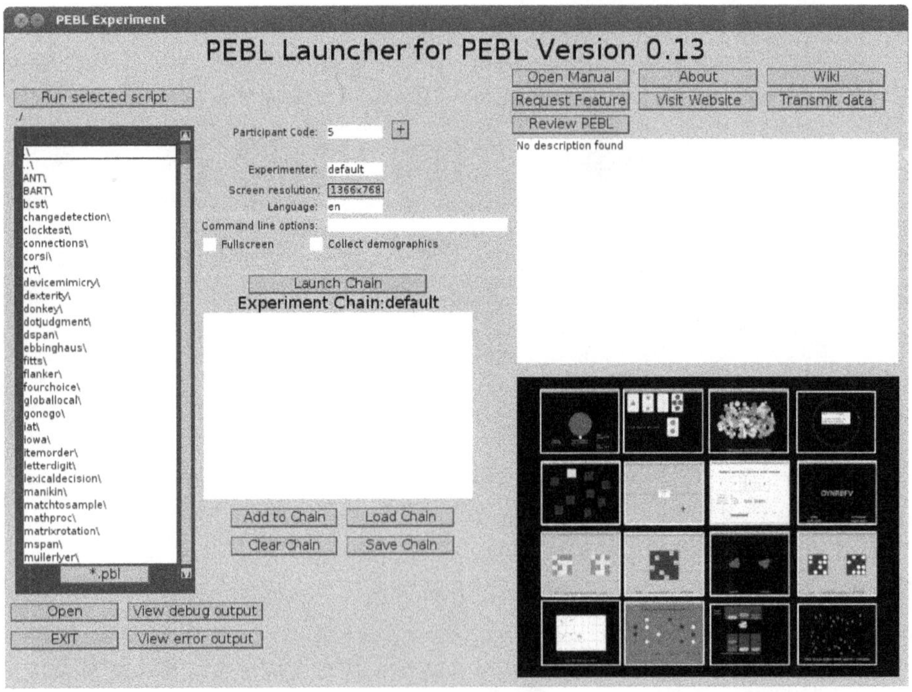

6.1   History of the Launcher

Prior to 2011, a front-end launcher was only available for PEBL on Windows. It was written in Visual Basic 6, which was old-fashioned, single-platform, no longer supported by Microsoft, and created a situation where a critical piece of PEBL infrastructure depended on a non-free tool. The main obstacle to a new launcher has always been: PEBL needs a cross-platform launcher using a free software, and we don't want to have to distribute a whole additional interpreter. This means that Python, wxBasic, TCL/TK, etc. were out of the consideration. Why couldn't there be an easy-to-use cross-platform programming tool we could use?

As of PEBL Version 0.12, we found one: PEBL itself. PEBL is not really designed to create GUI applications, but it can be beat into submission to do so. For Version 0.12, enough filesystem access functions and other features were available to make a reasonable launcher. Although the old-style launcher will probably still work, it will no longer be supported. The new launcher will not integrate completely seamlessly into your operating system, but it is designed to support the important functions of setting up and launching an experiment.

6.2   How it works

The simplest usage of the Launcher is that you use the file selector on the left to choose a .pbl file, then click the button 'Run selected script" to run that experiment. ONLY .pbl files and directories will appear in the file window.

6.3   Features

6.3.1   File browser

On the left is a file browser. It will
only show .pbl files and subdirectories. To navigate to a subdirectory,
simply click on the directory to select
it, then click on the selected directory.
To move back up a directory, click on
the '..\' row. When you have a .pbl
file selected, you can use the 'Run selected script' button to launch it.

6.3.2   Participant code

This will allow you to select the participant code you want sent to any experiments you are about to run. By
default, PEBL saves the last experiment code when you exit, and then
reloads it the next time, incrementing
by one. This makes it easier to avoid
colliding participant codes and over-
writing data. Participant code need
not be a number, but the launcher
currently does not understand how to

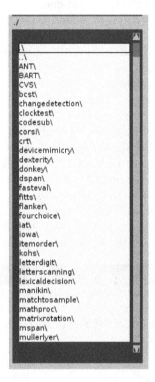

Figure 6.2: The PEBL Launcher File Browser.

increment non-numeric codes, and will probably restart at 1. The plus button
next to the code box will increment the current number by 1, which is useful if
you are running multiple sessions in a row.

The automatic incrementation of participant code can be turned off by opening
the fileselect.pbl file and changing the variable gAutoSubcode from 1 to 0.

When an experiment is launched, the specified code will be fed into the experiment using the -s command-line option, and will be bound to the gSubNum
variable. Some of the standard experiments will ask you to enter a participant
code regardless of whether you have one selected. If that is the case, you should
be able to edit the script to remove the request to specify a participant code.
However, most experiments in the test battery should only ask the experimenter
to specify a participant code if the participant code is '0', which is what it will
be when no -s command is given. So, if you are using code 0, many of the
experiments will ask you to enter a code after they launch.

6.3.3   Experimenter code

Many times, you may wish to keep track of the experimenter or research assistant
who collected the data. Have them enter their name in the 'experimenter'

window. The name will be saved on exit. The experimenter code will be saved to the runlog file (see below).

6.3.4 Language

Some experiments have instructions and stimuli that are translated into different languages. Enter your two-character language code in the language box to tell the experiment what language to use. If your chosen language is not available, the experiment will fall back to English. If you want to translate an experiment into your own language, ask on the PEBL mailing list.

6.3.5 Fullscreen Mode

If you want to launch your experiment in full-screen mode to improve video latency and to avoid distractions, check this box. The secret escape key combo is ctrl-alt-shift-\: hit these four to abort out of an experiment before it is complete.

6.3.6 Demographics Collection

The U.S. NIMH requires a number of demographic variables for research they fund. Checking this box will collect this data and save it to a data log file called demographics-log.csv, prior to running your experiment or experiment chain.

6.3.7 Experiment Chains

The launcher allows you to set up a 'chain' of experiments that get run in sequence. All the experiments will be run consecutively, with an identical subject code. This is accomplished by running a separate instance of PEBL for each experiment. The different experiments have no ability to communicate directly with one another.

6.3.8 Saving Experiment Chains

When you exit the launcher, the current experiment chain will get saved in the the current config file. By default, this file is called default.config. This same file is loaded when the launcher starts again, restoring your settings. In addition, a chain can be saved with a different name, and loaded, either at start-up (by specifying the name of the config file with the -v command-line option), or by entering the name in the dialog that occurs when 'Load Chain' is clicked.

6.3.9 Loading Experiment Chains

A previously saved experiment chain can be loaded using the 'load chain' button. If a config file with that name exists, it will load the settings and the experiment chain in that file. If no file exists with the specified name, it will change the name from 'default' (or whatever the current chain is called) to the specified

name, and save the current configuration to the new configuration file on exit
or when the 'save chain' button is clicked.

6.3.10 Description and Screenshot

On the right side of the launcher is a window that will show a screenshot and
print a description of a script when it is highlighted. These need to be created
by hand for each script.

6.3.11 Commmand Line Options

There are a number of command line options available for PEBL that are not
present as options in the launcher. If you want to use any, you can type them in
the "Command line Options" box and the launcher will pass them to PEBL. You
can use these to specify -V options that pass parameters into your experiment
(e.g., controlling whether a practice or a test round is given).

6.3.12 Other buttons

The launcher has a number of other buttons to help you use PEBL. These
include:

- *Open* On the lower left, there is a button labeled "Open". This will open
  a selected .pbl script in a text editor, and will open a directory in your
  system's file manager. An easy way to look at or make changes to the
  script, or to locate data files after a script is run.

- *View debug output* Whenever an experiment is run, any time you use the
  Print() function, it will print the resulting text to a file names stdout.txt
  the directory it was run in. This button will open that file.

- *View error output* Whenever an experiment is run, the error and status
  messages are saved to a file called stderr.txt in the directory it was run in.
  This button will open that file.

- *Exit* This will exit the launcher and save the current configuration options
  to the named experiment chain.

- *Open manual* This opens the PEBL .pdf manual. The manual is located in
  different places on each platform, and will change names for each release.

- *About* This provides a short description of the launcher.

- *Visit Website* This will take you to the main PEBL website.

- *Size* This lets you toggle the size of the launcher. The launcher screen
  by default is greater than 600 pixels high, which goes off the screen on
  some netbooks. Click this to change the default, then restart to use small
  window size.

- *Wiki* This button will take you to the PEBL wiki, and do its best to find a WIKI page related to the experiment you are looking at. They won't always exist, and if not, you can always sign in and make your own.

6.4 Launching an experiment

To launch an experiment, navigate through the directories in the file listing box. Only directories and files with the .pbl extension are shown in this box. To open a directory, click once to move the highlight box onto the directory name, and a second time to open the directory. When a new directory is opened, the first available .pbl file will be automatically selected. To run that script, just press the 'Run Selected script' button above the file select box. It will run with the specified parameter, including subject code, language, fullscreen mode. In addition, if the 'collect demographics' button is selected, a demographic survey will happen prior to the study running.

6.5 Launching an experiment chain

If you have a series of experiments you want to run, create an experiment chain and launch it using the 'Launch chain' button above the experiment chain selection box. Tip: Use experiment chains even if you are are running just single experiment, with just a single experiment selected. This give faster access and is less error-proned.

6.6 Translating the Launcher

You can translate the launcher to your own language. Open the launcher file (fileselect.pbl), and go to the end of the script, to a function named "GetStrings":

```
define GetStrings(lang)
{
   lang <- Uppercase(lang)
   if(lang == "EN")
   {
      gRunText <- "Run selected script"
      gOpenText <- "Open"
      gExitText <- "EXIT"
      gViewDebugText <- "View debug output"
      gViewErrorText <- "View error output"
      gAddToChainText <- "Add to Chain"
      gClearChainText <- "Clear Chain"
      gSaveChainText <- "Save Chain"
....
```

The labels used in the launcher all appear here. You should be able to just translate the text of each on into the language of your choice. Send the translations back to the author so they can be incorporated into the next launcher version. You can also make a section in the if statement for your particular language. When you change the language in launcher, it will save that option and use your language of choice next time.

Chapter 7

Detailed Function and Keyword Reference

7.1 Symbols

Name/Symbol: +

Description: Adds two expressions together. Also, concatenates strings together.

Usage:
```
<num1> + <num2>
<string1> + <string2>
<string1> + <num1>
```
Using other types of variables will cause errors.

Example:
```
33 + 322                  --> 355
"Hello" + " " + "World"   --> "Hello World"
"Hello" + 33 + 322.5      --> "Hello355.5"
33 + 322.5 + "Hello"      --> "33322.5Hello"
```

See Also: -, ToString()

Name/Symbol: -

Description: Subtracts one expression from another

Usage: `<num1> - <num2>`

Example:

See Also:

Name/Symbol: /

Description: Divides one expression by another

Usage: `<expression> / <expression>`

Example: `333 / 10    # == 33.3`

See Also:

Name/Symbol: *

Description: Multiplies two expressions together

Usage: `<expression> * <expression>`

Example: `32 * 2 # == 64`

See Also:

Name/Symbol: ^

Description: Raises one expression to the power of another expression

Usage: `<expression> ^ <expression>`

Example: `25 ^ 2  # == 625`

See Also: `Exp, NthRoot`

Name/Symbol: ;

Description: Finishes a statement, can start new statement on the same line (not needed at end of line)

Usage:

Example:

See Also:

Name/Symbol: #

Description: Comment indicator; anything until the next CR following this character is ignored

Usage:

Example:

See Also:

Name/Symbol: `<-`

Description: The assignment operator. Assigns a value to a variable
N.B.: This two-character sequence takes the place of the '=' operator found in many programming languages.

Usage:

Example:

See Also:

Name/Symbol: `( )`

Description: Groups mathematical operations

Usage: `(expression)`

Example: `(3 + 22) * 4  # == 100`

See Also:

Name/Symbol: `{ }`

Description: Groups a series of statements

Usage:
```
{ statement1
  statement2
  statement3
}
```

Example:

See Also:

Name/Symbol: `[ ]`

Description:	Creates a list. Closing] must be on same line as last element of list, even for nested lists.
Usage:	`[<item1>, <item2>, ....]`

Example:	`[]` `#Creates an empty list`
	`[1,2,3]` `#Simple list`
	`[[3,3,3],[2,2],0]` `#creates a nested list structure`

See Also:	`List()`

Name/Symbol:	<
Description:	Less than. Used to compare two numeric quantities.
Usage:	`3 < 5` `3 < value`

Example:	`if(j < 33)`
	`{`
	`   Print ("j is less than 33.")`
	`}`

	See Also: >, >=, <=, ==, ~=, !=, <>

Name/Symbol:	>
Description:	Greater than. Used to compare two numeric quantities.
Usage:	`5 > 3` `5 > value`

Example:	`if(j > 55)`
	`{`
	` Print ("j is greater than 55.")`
	`}`

See Also:	<, >=, <=, ==, ~=, !=, <>

Name/Symbol:	<=
Description:	Less than or equal to.
Usage:	`3<=5` `3<=value`

Example:
```
if(j <= 33)
{
 Print ("j is less than or equal to 33.")
}
```

See Also: <, >, >=, ==, ~=, !=, <>

Name/Symbol: >=

Description: Greater than or equal to.

Usage:
```
5>=3
5>=value
```

Example:
```
if(j >= 55)
{
 Print ("j is greater than or equal to 55.")
}
```

See Also: <, >, <=, ==, ~=, !=, <>

Name/Symbol: ==

Description: Equal to.

Usage: 4 == 4

Example: 2 + 2 == 4

See Also: <, >, >=, <=, ~=, !=, <>

Name/Symbol: <>, !=, ~=

Description: Not equal to.

Usage:

Example:

See Also: <, >, >=, <=, ==

7.2   A

Name/Symbol: `Abs()`

Description: Returns the absolute value of the number.

Usage: `Abs(<num>)`

Example: `Abs(-300)    # ==300`
                `Abs(23)      # ==23`

See Also: `Round()`, `Floor()`, `AbsFloor()`, `Sign()`, `Ceiling()`

Name/Symbol: `AbsFloor()`

Description: Rounds `<num>` toward 0 to an integer.

Usage: `AbsFloor(<num>)`

Example: `AbsFloor(-332.7)    # == -332`
                `AbsFloor(32.88)     # == 32`

See Also: `Round()`, `Floor()`, `Abs()`, `Sign()`, `Ceiling()`

Name/Symbol: `ACos()`

Description: Inverse cosine of `<num>`, in degrees.

Usage: `ACos(<num>)`

Example:

See Also: `Cos()`, `Sin()`, `Tan()`, `ATan()`, `ATan()`

Name/Symbol: `AddObject()`

Description: Adds a widget to a parent window, at the top of the object stack. Once added, the object will be drawn onto the parent last, meaning it will be on top of anything previously added.

In general, objects can be added to other objects as well as windows. For example, you can add drawing objects (circles, etc.) to an image to annotate the image and maintain its proper x,y coordinates.

Also, if you 're-add' an object that is already on a widget, it will get automatically removed from the window first. This is an easy way to reorder elements on a screen.

```
AddObject(<obj>, <window>)
AddObject(<obj>, <canvas>)
AddObject(<obj>, <widget>)
```

Example:

```
define Start(p)
{
 win <- MakeWindow()
 img <- MakeImage("pebl.png")
 circ <- Circle(20,20,10,MakeColor("red"),1)
 AddObject(circ,img)
 AddObject(img,win)
 Move(img,100,100)
 Draw()
 WaitForAnyKeyPress()
}
```

See Also: RemoveObject()

Name/Symbol: **and**

Description: Logical and operator.

Usage: `<expression> and <expression>`

Example:

See Also: or, **not**

Name/Symbol: **Append**

Description:	Appends an item to a list. Useful for constructing lists in conjunction with the loop statement.
	Note: `Append()` is useful, but inefficent for large data structures, because it requires making a copy of the entire data list and then overwriting it, if you use `list <- Append(list, item)`. The overhead will be hardly noticeable unless you are building lists hundreds of elements long. In that case you shuold either create the list upfront and use `SetElement`, or you `PushOnEnd` to modify the list directly.
Usage:	`Append(<list>, <item>)`

Example:

```
list <- Sequence(1,5,1)
double  <- []
loop(i, list)
{
 double <- Append(double, [i,i])
}
Print(double)
# Produces [[1,1],[2,2],[3,3],[4,4],[5,5]]
```

See Also:	`SetElement() List(), [ ], Merge(), PushOnEnd`

Name/Symbol:	`AppendFile`
Description:	Appends onto the end of `<file1>` the contents of `<file2>`. Useful for compiling pooled data at the end of an experiment.
Usage:	`AppendFile(<file1>, <file2>)`
Example:	:
	The following open ten consecutive files, writes 50 random numbers to each, then appends each to a master file:

```
loop(j, Sequence(1,10,1))
  {
    file <- FileOpenWrite(j+".txt")
  loop(i,Sequence(1,50,1))
    {
       FilePrint(file,j+","+i+","+Random())
    }
    AppendFile("master.txt",j+".txt")
  }
```

See Also:	`FileOpenWrite()`

Name/Symbol: `ASin()`

Description: Inverse Sine of `<num>`, in degrees.

Usage: `ASin(<num>)`

Example:

See Also: `Cos()`, `Sin()`, `Tan()`, `ATan()`, `ACos()`, `ATan()`

Name/Symbol: `ATan`

Description: Inverse Tan of `<num>`, in degrees.

Usage:

Example:

See Also: `Cos()`, `Sin()`, `Tan()`, `ATan()`, `ACos()`, `ATan()`

7.3 B

Name/Symbol: `Bezier`

Description: Creates a smoothed line through the points specified by `<xpoints>`, `<ypoints>`. The lists `<xpoints>` and `<ypoints>` are adjusted by `<x>` and `<y>`, so they should be relative to 0, not the location you want the points to be at.

Like other drawn objects, the bezier must then be added to the window to appear. ¡steps¿ denotes how smooth the approximation will be.

Usage:
```
Bezier(<x>,<y>,<xpoints>,<ypoints>,
       <steps>,<color>)
```

Example:
```
win <- MakeWindow()
 #This makes a T
 xpoints <- [-10,10,10,20,20,-20,-20,-10]
 ypoints <- [-20,-20,40,40,50,50,40,40]
p1 <-    Bezier(100,100,xpoints, ypoints,
          5, MakeColor("black"))
AddObject(p1,win)
Draw()
```

See Also: `BlockE(), Polygon(), MakeStarPoints(), MakeNGonPoints()`

Name/Symbol: `BlockE`

Description: Creates a polygon in the shape of a block E, pointing in one of four directions. Arguments include position in window.

- `<x>` and `<y>` is the position of the center
- `<h>` and `<w>` or the size of the E in pixels
- `<thickness>` thickness of the E
- `<direction>` specifies which way the E points: 1=right, 2=down, 3=left, 4=up.
- `<color>` is a color object (not just the name)

Like other drawn objects, the Block E must then be added to the window to appear.

Usage: `BlockE(x,y,h,w,thickness,direction,color)`

Example:
```
win <- MakeWindow()
e1 <- BlockE(100,100,40,80,10,1,MakeColor("black"))
AddObject(e1,win)
Draw()
```

See Also: Plus(), Polygon(), MakeStarPoints(), MakeNGonPoints()

Name/Symbol: `break`

Description: Breaks out of a loop immediately.

Usage: break

Example:
```
loop(i ,[1,3,5,9,2,7])
{
 Print(i)
 if(i == 3)
        {
         break
        }
}
```

See Also: `loop`, `return`

7.4   C

Name/Symbol: `Ceiling()`

Description: Rounds `<num>` up to the next integer.

Usage: `Ceiling(<num>)`

Example: `Ceiling(33.23)   # == 34`
`Ceiling(-33.02)  # == -33`

See Also: `Round()`, `Floor()`, `AbsFloor()`, `Ceiling()`

Name/Symbol: `ChooseN()`

Description: Samples `<number>` items from list, returning a list in the original order. Items are sampled without replacement, so once an item is chosen it will not be chosen again. If `<number>` is larger than the length of the list, the entire list is returned in order. It differs from `SampleN` in that `ChooseN` returns items in the order they appeared in the originial list, but `SampleN` is shuffled.

Usage: `ChooseN(<list>, <n>)`

Example:

```
# Returns 5 numbers
ChooseN([1,1,1,2,2], 5)

# Returns 3 numbers from 1 and 7:
ChooseN([1,2,3,4,5,6,7], 3)
```

See Also: `SampleN()`, `SampleNWithReplacement()`, `Subset()`

Name/Symbol: `Circle()`

Description: Creates a circle for graphing at x,y with radius r. Circles must be added to a parent widget before it can be drawn; it may be added to widgets other than a base window. The properties of circles may be changed by accessing their properties directly, including the FILLED property which makes the object an outline versus a filled shape.

Usage: `Circle(<x>, <y>, <r>,<color>)`

76

Example:

```
c <- Circle(30,30,20, MakeColor(green))
AddObject(c, win)
Draw()
```

See Also: Square(), Ellipse(), Rectangle(), Line()

Name/Symbol: CheckForNetworkConnection()

Description: Checks to see if there is an incoming TCP/IP connection on a network that is opened using OpenNetworkListener. This is an alternative to the WaitForNetworkConnection function that allows more flexibility (and allows updating the during waiting for the connection).

Usage: net <- CheckForNetwokConnection(network)

Example:
```
network <-        OpenNetworkListener(4444)
time <- GetTime()
while(not connected and (GetTime() < time + 5000))
  {
      connected <- CheckForNetwokConnection(network)
  }
```

See Also: OpenNetworkListener(),   Getdata(),
                WaitForNetworkConnection(), CloseNetwork()

Name/Symbol: ClearEventLoop()

Description: Clears the event loop. This function is currently experimental, and its usage may change in future versions of PEBL.

Usage: USAGE CURRENTLY UNDOCUMENTED

Example:

See Also: RegisterEvent(), StartEventLoop()

Name/Symbol: CloseNetworkConnection()

Description: Closes network connection

Usage: CloseNetwork(<network>)

Example:
```
net <- WaitForNetworkConnection("localhost",1234)
SendData(net,"Watson, come here. I need you.")
CloseNetworkConnection(net)
```

Also see nim.pbl for example of two-way network connection.

See Also: ConnectToIP, ConnectToHost, WaitForNetworkConnection, GetData, SendData, ConvertIPString

---

Name/Symbol: ConnectToHost()

Description: Connects to a host computer waiting for a connection on ¡port¿, returning a network object that can be used to communicate. Host is a text hostname, like "myname.indiana.edu", or use "localhost" to specify your current computer.

Usage: ConnectToHost(<hostname>,<port>)

Example: See nim.pbl for example of two-way network connection.

```
net <- ConnectToHost("localhost",1234)
dat <- GetData(net,20)
Print(dat)
CloseNetworkConnection(net)
```

See Also: ConnectToIP, GetData, WaitForNetworkConnection, SendData, ConvertIPString, CloseNetworkConnection

---

Name/Symbol: ConnectToIP()

Description: Connects to a host computer waiting for a connection on <port>, returning a network object that can be used to communicate. <ip> is a numeric ip address, which must be created with the ConvertIPString(ip) function.

Usage: ConnectToIP(<ip>,<port>)

Example: See nim.pbl for example of two-way network connection.

```
ip <- ConvertIPString("192.168.0.1")
net <- ConnectToHost(ip,1234)
dat <- GetData(net,20)
Print(dat)
CloseNetworkConnection(net)
```

See Also: ConnectToHost, GetData, WaitForNetworkConnection, SendData, ConvertIPString, CloseNetworkConnection

Name/Symbol: `ConvertIPString()`

Description: Converts an IP address specified as a string into an integer that can be used by ConnectToIP.

Usage: `ConvertIPString(<ip-as-string>)`

Example: See nim.pbl for example of two-way network connection.

```
ip <- ConvertIPString("192.168.0.1")
net <- ConnectToHost(ip,1234)
dat <- GetData(net,20)
Print(dat)
CloseNetworkConnection(net)
```

See Also: ConnectToHost, ConnectToIP, GetData, WaitForNetworkConnection, SendData, CloseNetworkConnection

---

Name/Symbol: `ConvexHull()`

Description: Computes the convex hull of a set of [x,y] points. It returns a set of points that forms the convex hull, with the first and last point identical. A convex hull is the set of outermost points, such that a polygon connecting just those points will encompass all other points, and such that no angle is acute. It is used in MakeAttneave.

Usage: `ConvexHull(<list-of-x-y-points>)`

Example:
```
pts <- [[0.579081, 0.0327737],
        [0.0536094, 0.378258],
        [0.239628, 0.187751],
        [0.940625, 0.26526],
        [0.508748, 0.840846],
        [0.352604, 0.200193],
        [0.38684, 0.212413],
        [0.00114761, 0.768165],
        [0.432963, 0.629412]]
Print(ConvexHull(pts))
```

output:

```
[[0.940625, 0.26526]
, [0.508748, 0.840846]
, [0.00114761, 0.768165]
, [0.0536094, 0.378258]
, [0.239628, 0.187751]
, [0.579081, 0.0327737]
, [0.940625, 0.26526]
```

See Also: MakeAttneave,

Name/Symbol: Cos()

Description: Cosine of <deg> degrees.

Usage:

Example: Cos(33.5)
               Cos(-32)

See Also: Sin(), Tan(), ATan(), ACos(), ATan()

Name/Symbol: Countdown()

Description: Displays a 3-2-1 countdown on the screen in with 500 ms ISI.
               CountDown temporarily hides whatever is on the screen. It is
               useful in orienting participants to the first trial of a task.

Usage: CountDown(win)

Example: win <- MakeWindow()
               MessageBox("Press any key to begin",win)
               CountDown(win)
               Trial()

See Also: MessageBox

Name/Symbol: CR()

Description: Produces <number> linefeeds which can be added to a string and
               printed or saved to a file. CR is an abbreviation for "Carriage
               Return".

Usage: CR(<number>)

Example:
```
Print("Number: "  Tab(1) + number  + CR(2))
Print("We needed space before this line.")
```

See Also: Format(), Tab()

Name/Symbol: CrossFactorWithoutDuplicates()

Description: This function takes a single list, and returns a list of all pairs, excluding the pairs that have two of the same item. To achieve the same effect but include the duplicates, use: DesignFullCounterBalance(x,x).

Usage: CrossFactorWithoutDuplicates(<list>)

Example:
```
CrossFactorWithoutDuplicates([a,b,c])
# == [[a,b],[a,c],[b,a],[b,c],[c,a],[c,b]]
```

See Also: DesignFullCounterBalance(), Repeat(), DesignBalancedSampling(), DesignGrecoLatinSquare(), DesignLatinSquare(), RepeatList(), LatinSquare(), Shuffle()

Name/Symbol: CumNormInv()

Description: This function takes a probability and returns the corresponding z-score for the cumulative standard normal distribution. It uses an accurate numerical approximation from: http://home.online.no/ pjacklam/notes/invnorm

Usage: CumNormInv(<p>)

Example:
```
Print(CumNormInv(0))    #= NA
 Print(CumNormInv(.01)) #= -2.32634
 Print(CumNormInv(.5))  #= 0
 Print(CumNormInv(.9))  #= 1.28
 Print(CumNormInv(1))   #= NA
```

See Also: NormalDensity(), RandomNormal()

7.5 D

Name/Symbol: `define`

Description: Defines a user-specified function.

Usage:
```
define functionname (parameters)
{
 statement1
 statement2
 statement3
        #Return statement is optional:
 return <value>
}
```

Example: See above.

See Also:

Name/Symbol: `DegToRad()`

Description: Converts degrees to radians.

Usage: `DegToRad(<deg>)`

Example: `DegToRad(180) # == 3.14159...`

See Also: `Cos(), Sin(), Tan(), ATan(), ACos(), ATan()`

Name/Symbol: `DesignBalancedSampling()`

Description: Samples elements "roughly" equally. This function returns a list of repeated samples from `<treatment_list>`, such that each element in `<treatment_list>` appears approximately equally. Each element from `<treatment_list>` is sampled once without replacement before all elements are returned to the mix and sampling is repeated. If there are no repeated items in `<list>`, there will be no consecutive repeats in the output. The last repeat-sampling will be truncated so that a `<length>`-size list is returned. If you don't want the repeated epochs this function provides, Shuffle() the results.

Usage: `DesignBalancedSampling(<list>, <length>)`

Example:
```
DesignBalancedSampling([1,2,3,4,5],12)
## e.g., produces something like:
##    [5,3,1,4,2, 3,1,5,2,4, 3,1 ]
```

See Also:
```
CrossFactorWithoutDuplicates(), Shuffle(),
DesignFullCounterBalance(), DesignGrecoLatinSquare(),
DesignLatinSquare(), Repeat(), RepeatList(),
LatinSquare()
```

Name/Symbol: `DesignFullCounterbalance()`

Description: This takes two lists as parameters, and returns a nested list of lists that includes the full counterbalancing of both parameter lists. Use cautiously; this gets very large.

Usage:
```
DesignFullCounterbalance(<lista>, <listb>)
```

Example:
```
a <- [1,2,3]
b <- [9,8,7]
DesignFullCounterbalance(a,b)
# == [[1,9],[1,8],[1,7],
#     [2,9],[2,8],[2,7],
#     [3,9],[3,8],[3,7]]
```

See Also:
```
CrossFactorWithoutDuplicates(),          LatinSquare(),
Shuffle(), DesignBalancedSampling(),
DesignGrecoLatinSquare(),          DesignLatinSquare(),
Repeat(), RepeatList(),
```

Name/Symbol: `DesignGrecoLatinSquare()`

Description: This will return a list of lists formed by rotating through each element of the `<treatment_list>`s, making a list containing all element of the list, according to a greco-latin square. All lists must be of the same length.

Usage:
```
DesignGrecoLatinSquare(<factor_list>,
                       <treatment_list>,
                       <treatment_list>)
```

Example:
```
x <- ["a","b","c"]
y <- ["p","q","r"]
z <- ["x","y","z"]
Print(DesignGrecoLatinSquare(x,y,z))
# produces:    [[[a, p, x], [b, q, y], [c, r, z]],
#               [[a, q, z], [b, r, x], [c, p, y]],
#               [[a, r, y], [b, p, z], [c, q, x]]]
```

83

See Also: `CrossFactorWithoutDuplicates()`, `LatinSquare()`,
             `DesignFullCounterBalance()`, `DesignBalancedSampling()`,
             `DesignLatinSquare()`, `Repeat()`, `RepeatList()`, `Shuffle()`

Name/Symbol: `DesignLatinSquare()`

Description: This returns return a list of lists formed by rotating through
              each element of `<treatment_list>`, making a list containing
              all element of the list. Has no side effect on input lists.

Usage: `DesignLatinSquare(<treatment1_list>,`
                               `<treatment2_list>)`

Example:
```
order <- [1,2,3]
treatment <- ["A","B","C"]
design <- DesignLatinSquare(order,treatment)
# produces: [[[1, A], [2, B], [3, C]],
#            [[1, B], [2, C], [3, A]],
#            [[1, C], [2, A], [3, B]]]
```

See Also: `CrossFactorWithoutDuplicates()`,
             `DesignFullCounterBalance()`, `DesignBalancedSampling()`,
             `DesignGrecoLatinSquare()`,   `Repeat()`,   `LatinSquare()`
             `RepeatList()`, `Shuffle()`, `Rotate()`

Name/Symbol: `Dist()`

Description: Returns Euclidean distance between two points. Each point
              should be [x,y], and any additional items in the list are ignored.

Usage: `Dist(<xylist1>, <xylist2>)`

Example:
```
p1 <- [0,0]
p2 <- [3,4]
d <- Dist(p1,p2)  #d is 5
```

See Also:

Name/Symbol: `Div()`

Description: Returns round(`<num>`/`<mod>`)

Usage: `Div(<num>, <mod>)`

Example:

See Also: `Mod()`

Name/Symbol: `Draw()`

Description: Redraws the screen or a specific widget.

Usage: `Draw()`
                `Draw(<object>)`

Example:

See Also: `DrawFor()`, `Show()`, `Hide()`

Name/Symbol: `DrawFor()`

Description: Draws a screen or widget, returning after `<cycles>` refreshes.
                This function currently does not work as intended in the SDL
                implementation, because of a lack of control over the refresh
                blank. It may work in the future.

Usage: `DrawFor( <object>, <cycles>)`

Example:

See Also: `Draw()`, `Show()`, `Hide()`

7.6   E

Name/Symbol: `EasyLabel()`

Description: Creates and adds to the window location a label at specified location. Uses standard vera font with grey background. (May in the future get background color from window). Easy-to-use replacement for the `MakeFont`, `MakeLabel`, `AddObject`, `Move`, steps you typically have to go through.

Usage: `EasyLabel( <text>,<x>, <y>, <win>, <fontsize>)`

Example:
```
win <- MakeWindow()
lab <- EasyLabel("What?",200,100,win,12)
Draw()
```

See Also: `EasyTextBox()`, `MakeLabel()`

Name/Symbol: `EasyTextBox()`

Description: Creates and adds to the window location a textbox at specified location. Uses standard vera font with white background. Easy-to-use replacement for the MakeFont,MakeTextBox, AddObject, Move, steps.

Usage: `EasyTextBox( <text>,<x>, <y>, <win>,`
`                    <fontsize>,<width>,<height>)`

Example:
```
win <- MakeWindow()
entry <- EasyTextBox("1 2 3 4 5",200,100,
                           win,12,200,50)
Draw()
```

See Also: `EasyLabel()`, `MakeTextBox()`

Name/Symbol: `Ellipse()`

Description: Creates a ellipse for graphing at x,y with radii rx and ry. Ellipses are only currently definable oriented in horizontal/vertical directions. Ellipses must be added to a parent widget before it can be drawn; it may be added to widgets other than a base window. The properties of ellipses may be changed by accessing their properties directly, including the FILLED property which makes the object an outline versus a filled shape.

Usage: `Ellipse(<x>, <y>, <rx>, <ry>,<color>)`

Example:

```
e <- Ellipse(30,30,20,10, MakeColor(green))
AddObject(e, win)
Draw()
```

See Also: `Square(), Circle(), Rectangle(), Line()`

Name/Symbol: `EndOfFile()`

Description: Returns true if at the end of a file.

Usage: `EndOfFile(<filestream>)`

Example:
```
while(not EndOfFile(fstream))
{
 Print(FileReadLine(fstream))
}
```
See Also:

Name/Symbol: `EndOfLine()`

Description: Returns true if at end of line.

Usage: `EndOfLine(<filestream>)`

Example:

See Also:

Name/Symbol: `Enquote()`

Description: Surrounds the argument with quotes.

Usage: `Enquote("one two three")`

Example:
```
##use to add quoted text to instructions.
instructions <- "Respond whenever you see an "+
                 Enquote("X")

##Use it for saving data that may have spaces:
resp <-  GetInput(tb, "<enter>")
FilePrint(fileout, Enquote(resp))
```

See Also: gQuote

Name/Symbol: Exp()

Description: *e* to the power of <pow>.

Usage: Exp(<pow>)

Example: Exp(0) # == 1
              Exp(3) # == 20.0855

See Also: Log()

Name/Symbol: ExtractListItems()

Description: Extracts items from a list, forming a new list. The list <items>
              are the integers representing the indices that should be ex-
              tracted.

Usage: ExtractListItems(<list>,<items>)

Example: myList <- Sequence(101, 110, 1)
              ExtractListItems(myList, [2,4,5,1,4])
              # produces [102, 104, 105, 101, 104]

See Also: Subset(), SubList(), SampleN()

7.7   F

Name/Symbol: `FileClose()`

Description: Closes a filestream variable. Be sure to pass the variable name, not the filename.

Usage: `FileClose(<filestream>)`

Example:
```
x <- FileOpenRead("file.txt")
# Do relevant stuff here.
FileClose(x)
```

See Also: `FileOpenAppend()`, `FileOpenRead()`, `FileOpenWrite()`

Name/Symbol: `FileExists()`

Description: Checks whether a file exists. Returns 1 if it exists, 0 otherwise.

Usage: `FileExists(<path>)`

Example:
```
filename <- "data-"+gSubNum+".csv"
exists <-  FileExists(filename)
 if(exists)
   {
    MessageBox("Subject file already exists.  Please try a new one.",gWin)
    SignalFatalError("filename already used")
   }
```

See Also: `GetDirectoryListing()`, `FileExists()`, `IsDirectory()`, `MakeDirectory()`

Name/Symbol: `FileOpenAppend()`

Description: Opens a filename, returning a stream that can be used for writing information. Appends if the file already exists.

Usage: `FileOpenAppend(<filename>)`

Example:

See Also: `FileClose()`,   `FileOpenRead()`,   `FileOpenWrite()`, `FileOpenOverWrite()`

Name/Symbol: `FileOpenOverwrite()`

Description: Opens a filename, returning a stream that can be used for writing information. Overwrites if file already exists. This function should not be used for opening data files; instead, use FileOpen-Write, which saves to a backup file if the specified file already exists.

Usage: `FileOpenOverWrite(<filename>)`

Example:

See Also: `FileClose()`, `FileOpenAppend()`, `FileOpenRead()` `FileOpenWrite()`

Name/Symbol: `FileOpenRead()`

Description: Opens a filename, returning a stream to be used for reading information.

Usage: `FileOpenRead(<filename>)`

Example:

See Also: `FileClose()`, `FileOpenAppend()`, `FileOpenWrite()`, `FileOpenOverWrite()`

Name/Symbol: `FileOpenWrite()`

Description: Opens a filename, returning a stream that can be used for writing information. If the specified filename exists, it won't overwrite that file. Instead, it will create a related filename, appending a -integer before the filename extension.

Usage: `FileOpenWrite(<filename>)`

Example: In the following example, test.txt gets created with the text "testing 1", and then a second file test-1.txt gets created with the text "testing 2".

```
f1 <- FileOpenWrite("test.txt")
FilePrint(f1,"testing 1")
FileClose(f1)
f2 <- FileOpenWrite("test.txt")
FilePrint(f2,"testing 2")
FileClose(f2)
```

See Also: `FileClose()`, `FileOpenAppend()`, `FileOpenRead()`, `FileOpenOverWrite()`

Name/Symbol: `FilePrint()`

Description: Like `Print`, but to a file. Prints a string to a file, with a carriage return at the end. Returns a copy of the string it prints.

Usage: `FilePrint(<filestream>, <value>)`

Example: `FilePrint(fstream, "Another Line.")`

See Also: `Print()`, `FilePrint_()`

Name/Symbol: `FilePrint_()`

Description: Like `Print_`, but to a file. Prints a string to a file, without appending a newline character. Returns a copy of the string it prints.

Usage: `FilePrint_(<filestream>, <value>)`

Example: `FilePrint_(fstream, "This line doesn't end.")`

See Also: `Print_()`, `FilePrint()`

Name/Symbol: `FilePrintList()`

Description: Prints a list to a file, without the ','s or [] characters. Puts a carriage return at the end. Returns a string that was printed. If a list contains other lists, the printing will wrap multiple lines and the internal lists will be printed as normal. To avoid this, try FilePrintList(file,Flatten(list)).

Usage: `FilePrintList(<filestream>, <list>)`

Example:

```
FilePrintList(fstream, [1,2,3,4,5,5,5])
##
##  Produces:
##1 2 3 4 5 5 5
FilePrintList(fstream,[[1,2],[3,4],[5,6]])
#Produces:
# [1,2]
#,[3,4]
```

```
#,[5,6]

FilePrintList(fstream,Flatten([[1,2],[3,4],[5,6]]))
#Produces:
# 1 2 3 4 5 6
```

See Also: Print(),   Print_(),   FilePrint(),   FilePrint_(),
                 PrintList(),

Name/Symbol: `FileReadCharacter()`

Description: Reads and returns a single character from a filestream.

Usage: `FileReadCharacter(<filestream>)`

Example:

See Also: `FileReadList()`,   `FileReadTable()`   `FileReadLine()`,
                 `FileReadText()`, `FileReadWord()`,

Name/Symbol: `FileReadLine()`

Description: Reads and returns a line from a file; all characters up until the next newline or the end of the file.

Usage: `FileReadLine(<filestream>)`

Example:

See Also: `FileReadCharacter()`,`FileReadList()`,   `FileReadTable()`
                 `FileReadText()`, `FileReadWord()`,

Name/Symbol: `FileReadList()`

Description: Given a filename, will open it, read in all the items into a list (one item per line), and close the file afterward. Ignores blank lines or lines starting with #. Useful with a number of pre-defined data files stored in **media/text/**. See Section 4.17.4: Provided Media Files.

Usage: `FileReadList(<filename>)`

Example: `FileReadList("data.txt")`

See Also: FileReadCharacter(), FileReadTable() FileReadLine(),
                 FileReadText(), FileReadWord(),

Name/Symbol: FileReadTable()

Description: Reads a table directly from a file. Data in file should separated
                 by spaces. Reads each line onto a sublist, with space-separated
                 tokens as items in sublist. Ignores blank lines or lines beginning
                 with #. Optionally, specify a token separator other than space.

Usage: FileReadTable(<filename>, <optional-separator>)

Example: a <- FileReadTable("data.txt")

See Also: FileReadCharacter(),FileReadList(),   FileReadLine(),
                 FileReadText(), FileReadWord(),

Name/Symbol: FileReadText()

Description: Returns all of the text from a file, ignoring any lines beginning
                 with #. Opens and closes the file transparently.

Usage: FileReadText(<filename>)

Example: instructions <- FileReadText("instructions.txt")

See Also: FileReadCharacter(),FileReadList(),   FileReadTable()
                 FileReadLine(), FileReadWord(),

Name/Symbol: FileReadWord()

Description: Reads and returns a 'word' from a file; the next connected
                 stream of characters not including a ' ' or a newline. Will
                 not read newline characters.

Usage: FileReadWord(<filestream>)

Example:

See Also: FileReadLine(),   FileReadTable(),   FileReadList()
                 FileReadCharacter(),FileReadList(),   FileReadTable()
                 FileReadLine(), FileReadText(), FileReadWord(),

---

Name/Symbol: Filter()

Description: Returns a subset of `<list>`, depending on whether the `<filter>` list is zero or nonzero. Both arguments must be lists of the same length.

Usage: `Filter(<list>,<filter>)`

Example:
```
x <- [1,2,3,3,2,2,1]
Print(Filter(x,[1,1,1,0,0,0,0])) ##==[1,2,3]
Print(Filter(x,Match(x,1)))      ##== [1,1]
```

See Also: `Match()`, `Subset()`, `Lookup()`

Name/Symbol: `FindInString()`

Description: Finds a token in a string, returning the position.

Usage: `FindInString(<string>,<string>)`

Example: `FindInString("about","bo")  # == 2`

See Also: `SplitString()`

Name/Symbol: `First()`

Description: Returns the first item of a list.

Usage: `First(<list>)`

Example: `First([3,33,132]) # == 3`

See Also: `Nth()`, `Last()`

Name/Symbol: `Flatten()`

Description: Flattens nested list `<list>` to a single flat list.

Usage: `Flatten(<list>)`

Example:
```
Flatten([1,2,[3,4],[5,[6,7],8],[9]])
# == [1,2,3,4,5,6,7,8,9]
Flatten([1,2,[3,4],[5,[6,7],8],[9]])
# == [1,2,3,4,5,6,7,8,9]
```

See Also: `FlattenN()`, `FoldList()`

Name/Symbol: `FlattenN()`

Description: Flattens `<n>` levels of nested list `<list>`.

Usage: `Flatten(<list>, <n>)`

Example: `Flatten([1,2,[3,4],[5,[6,7],8],[9]],1)`
`# == [1,2,3,4,5,[6,7],8,9]`

See Also: `Flatten(), FoldList()`

Name/Symbol: `Floor()`

Description: Rounds `<num>` down to the next integer.

Usage: `Floor(<num>)`

Example: `Floor(33.23) # == 33`
`Floor(3.999)   # ==3`
`Floor(-32.23)  # == -33`

See Also: `AbsFloor(), Round(), Ceiling()`

Name/Symbol: `FoldList()`

Description: Folds a list into equal-length sublists.

Usage: `FoldList(<list>, <size>)`

Example: `FoldList([1,2,3,4,5,6,7,8],2)`
`# == [[1,2],[3,4],[5,6],[7,8]]`

See Also: `FlattenN(), Flatten()`

Name/Symbol: `Format()`

Description: Formats the printing of values to ensure the proper spacing. It will either truncate or pad `<value>` with spaces so that it ends up exactly `<length>` characters long. Character padding is at the end.

Usage: `Format(<value>, <length>)`

Example:

```
x <- 33.23425225
y <- 23.3
Print("["+Format(x,5)+"]")
Print("["+Format(y,5)+"]")
## Output:
## [33.23 ]
## [23.3  ]
```

See Also: CR() Tab()

7.8 G

Name/Symbol: GetAngle()

Description: Gets an angle (in degrees) from (0,0) of an x,y coordinate

Usage: GetAngle(<x>,<y>)

Example:
```
##point sprite in the direction of a click
sprite <- LoadImage("car.png")
AddObject(sprite,gWin)
Move(sprite,300,300)
xy <- WaitForDownClick()
newangle <- GetAngle(First(xy)-300,Second(xy)-300)
sprite.rotation <- newangle
Draw()
```

See Also: DegtoRad, RadToDeg

Name/Symbol: GetAngle3()

Description: Gets an angle (in radians) of abc.

Usage: GetAngle3(<a>,<b>,<c>)

Example:
```
a <- [0.579081, 0.0327737]
b <- [0.0536094, 0.378258]
c <- [0.239628, 0.187751]

Print(GetAngle3(a,b,c)) ## .2157
```

See Also: DegtoRad, RadToDeg, GetAngle, ToRight

Name/Symbol: GetCurrentScreenResolution()

Description: Returns an list of [width,height] specifying what the current computer screen resolution is. This is used within the pebl launcher in order to use the current resolution to run the experiment.

Usage: res <- GetCurrentScreenResolution()

Example:
```
define Start(p)
{
  ## For testing, let's make the screen resolution a bit smaller than th
  ## current one so that it doesn't get hidden by the bottom task bar
  ##
  res <- GetCurrentScreenResolution()
  gVideoWidth <- First(res)-100
  gVideoHeight <- Second(res)-100
  gWin <- MakeWindow()
  MessageBox("Window slightly smaller than screen",gWin)
}
```

See Also: `GetVideoModes()`

Name/Symbol: `GetCursorPosition()`

Description: Returns an integer specifying where in a textbox the edit cursor is. The value indicates which character it is on.

Usage: `GetCursorPosition(<textbox>)`

Example:

See Also: `SetCursorPosition(), MakeTextBox(), SetText()`

Name/Symbol: `GetData()`

Description: Gets Data from network connection. Example of usage in demo/nim.pbl.

Usage: `val <- GetData(<network>,<size>)`

Example: On 'server':

```
net <- WaitForNetworkConnection("localhost",1234)
SendData(net,"Watson, come here. I need you.")
value <-  GetData(net,10)
Print(value)
```

On Client:

```
net <- ConnectToHost("localhost",1234)
value <-  GetData(net,20)
Print(value)
##should print out "Watson, come here. I need you."
```

98

See Also: `ConnectToIP, ConnectToHost, WaitForNetworkConnection, SendData, ConvertIPString, CloseNetworkConnection`

Name/Symbol: `GetDirectoryListing()`

Description: Returns a list of files and directories in a particular directory/folder.

Usage: `list <- GetDirectoryListing(<path>)`

Example: `files <- GetDirectoryListing("./")`

See Also: `GetDirectoryListing(), FileExists(), IsDirectory(), MakeDirectory()`

Name/Symbol: `GetEasyChoice()`

Description: Hides what is on the screen and presents a textbox with specified message, and a series of options to select from. Returns element from corresponding position of the `<output>` list.

Usage:
```
GetEasyChoice(<message>,<list-of-choices>,
              <output>,<window>)
```

Example: The code snippet below produces the following screen:

```
gWin <- MakeWindow("white")
inp <- GetEasyChoice("What Year are you in school",
                ["First-year","Sophomore",
                "Junior","Senior","Other"],
                [1,2,3,4,5], gWin)
```

See Also: MessageBox,GetEasyChoice, EasyTextBox

Name/Symbol: `GetEasyInput()`

Description: Hides what is on the screen and presents a textbox with specified message, and a second text box to enter input. Continues when 'enter' it hit at the end of text entry.

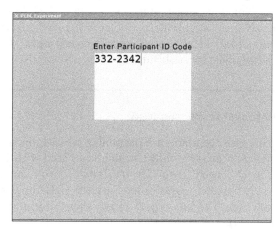

Usage:

GetEasyInput(<message>,<window>)

Example: gWin <- MakeWindow()
            inp <- GetEasyInput("Enter Participant ID Code",gWin)

See Also: MessageBox() GetEasyChoice(), EasyTextBox()

Name/Symbol: `GetInput()`

Description: Allows user to type input into a textbox.

Usage: GetInput(<textbox>,<escape-key>)

Example:

See Also: SetEditable(), GetCursorPosition(), MakeTextBox(),
             SetText()

Name/Symbol: `GetJoystickAxisState`

Description: This gets the state of a particular joystick axis. You need to specify a joystick object, which is created with OpenJoystick(). You also need to specify the axis. You can determine how many axes a joystick has with the GetNumJoystickAxes() function. The function returns a value between 1 and 32768.

Usage: `GetJoystickAxisState(js,1)`

Example: See joysticktest.pbl in the demo directory

See Also: GetNumJoysticks(), OpenJoystick(), GetNumJoystickAxes() GetNumJoystickBalls(), GetNumJoystickButtons(), Get-NumJoystickHats() GetJoystickAxisState(), GetJoystickHat-State(), GetJoystickButtonState()

Name/Symbol: `GetJoystickButtonState`

Description: This gets the state of a particular joystick button. You need to specify a joystick object, which is created with OpenJoystick(). You also need to specify the button. You can determine how many buttons a joystick has with the GetNumJoystickButtons() function. The function returns either 0 (for unpressed) or 1 (for pressed).

Usage: `GetJoystickButtonState(js,1)`

Example: See joysticktest.pbl in the demo directory

See Also: GetNumJoysticks(), OpenJoystick(), GetNumJoystickAxes() GetNumJoystickBalls(), GetNumJoystickButtons(), Get-NumJoystickHats() GetJoystickAxisState(), GetJoystickHat-State(), GetJoystickButtonState()

Name/Symbol: `GetJoystickBallState`

Description: Not implemented.

Usage: `GetJoystickBallState(js,1)`

Example: See joysticktest.pbl in the demo directory

See Also: GetNumJoysticks(), OpenJoystick(), GetNumJoystickAxes() GetNumJoystickBalls(), GetNumJoystickButtons(), Get-NumJoystickHats() GetJoystickAxisState(), GetJoystickHat-State(), GetJoystickButtonState()

Name/Symbol: `GetJoystickHatState`

Description:

Usage: `GetJoystickHatState(js,1)` This gets the state of a particular joystick hat. You need to specify a joystick object, which is created with OpenJoystick(). You also need to specify the hat id. You can determine how many hats a joystick has with the GetNumJoystickHats() function. The function returns a value between 0 and 15, which is the sum of values specifying whether each primary NSEW direction is pressed. The coding is: 0=no buttons; 1=N, 2=E, 4=S, 8=W. Thus, if 1 is returned, the north hat button is pressed. If 3 is returned, NorthEast. If 12 is returned, SW, and so on.

Example: See joysticktest.pbl in the demo directory

See Also: GetNumJoysticks(), OpenJoystick(), GetNumJoystickAxes() GetNumJoystickBalls(), GetNumJoystickButtons(), Get-NumJoystickHats() GetJoystickAxisState(), GetJoystickHat-State(), GetJoystickButtonState()

Name/Symbol: `GetMouseCursorPosition()`

Description: Gets the current x,y coordinates of the mouse pointer.

Usage: `GetMouseCursorPosition()`

Example:

`pos <- GetMouseCursorPosition()`

See Also: `ShowCursor,` `WaitForMouseButton,` `SetMouseCursorPosition, GetMouseCursorPosition`

Name/Symbol: `GetMouseState()`

Description: Gets the current x,y coordinates of the mouse pointer, plus the current state of the buttons. Returns a 5-element list, with the first two indicating x,y position, the third is either 0 or 1 depending on if the left mouse is clicked, the fourth 0 or 2 depending on whether the middle mouse is clicked, and the fifth either 0 or 4 depending on whether the right mouse is clicked.

Usage: `GetMouseState()`

Example:
```
define Start(p)
{

  win <- MakeWindow()
  i <- 1
  while(i < 100)
  {
    Draw()
    Print(GetMouseState())

    Wait(100)
    i <- i + 1

  }
##Returns look like:
[417, 276, 0, 0, 0]
[495, 286, 0, 0, 0]
[460, 299, 0, 0, 0]
[428, 217, 0, 0, 0]
[446, 202, 0, 0, 4]
[446, 202, 1, 0, 0]
[446, 202, 1, 0, 0]
[446, 202, 0, 2, 0]
```

See Also: ShowCursor WaitForMouseButton, SetMouseCursorPosition,
              GetMouseCursorPosition

Name/Symbol: `GetNIMHDemographics()`

Description: Gets demographic information that are normally required for
                NIMH-related research. Currently are gender (M/F/prefer not
                to say), ethnicity (Hispanic or not), and race (A.I./Alaskan,
                Asian/A.A., Hawaiian, black/A.A., white/Caucasian, other). It
                then prints their responses in a single line in the demographics
                file, along with any special code you supply and a time/date
                stamp. This code might include a subject number, experiment
                number, or something else, but many informed consent forms
                assure the subject that this information cannot be tied back to
                them or their data, so be careful about what you record. The
                file output will look something like:

```
----

31,Thu May 12 17:00:35 2011,F,hisp,asian,3331
32,Thu May 12 22:49:10 2011,M,nothisp,amind,3332
----
```

The first column is the user-specified code (in this case, indicating the experiment number). The middle columns indicate date/time, and the last three columns indicate gender (M, F, other), Hispanic (Y/N), and race.

Usage: `GetNIMHDemographics(<code-to-print-out>,`
                              `<window>, <filename>)`

Example: `GetNIMHDemographics("x0413", gwindow,`
                              `"x0413-demographics.txt")`

See Also:

Name/Symbol: `GetNumJoystickAxes`

Description: This gets the number of axes on a joystick. You need to specify a joystick object, which is created with OpenJoystick().

Usage: `GetNumJoystickAxes(js,1)`

Example: See joysticktest.pbl in the demo directory

See Also: GetNumJoysticks(), OpenJoystick(), GetNumJoystickAxes() GetNumJoystickBalls(), GetNumJoystickButtons(), GetNumJoystickHats() GetJoystickAxisState(), GetJoystickHatState(), GetJoystickButtonState()

Name/Symbol: `GetNumJoystickBalls`

Description: This gets the number of joystick balls available on a particular joystick. You need to specify a joystick object, which is created with OpenJoystick().

Usage: `GetNumJoystickBalls(js)`

Example: See joysticktest.pbl in the demo directory

See Also: GetNumJoysticks(), OpenJoystick(), GetNumJoystickAxes() GetNumJoystickBalls(), GetNumJoystickButtons(), GetNumJoystickHats() GetJoystickAxisState(), GetJoystickHatState(), GetJoystickButtonState()

Name/Symbol: `GetNumJoystickButtons`

Description: This gets the number of joystick buttons available on a particular joystick. You need to specify a joystick object, which is created with OpenJoystick().

Usage: `GetNumJoystickButtons(js,1)`

Example: See joysticktest.pbl in the demo directory

See Also: GetNumJoysticks(), OpenJoystick(), GetNumJoystickAxes() GetNumJoystickBalls(), GetNumJoystickButtons(), GetNumJoystickHats() GetJoystickAxisState(), GetJoystickHatState(), GetJoystickButtonState()

Name/Symbol: `GetNumJoystickHats`

Description: This gets the number of hats available on a particular joystick. You need to specify a joystick object, which is created with OpenJoystick().

Usage: `GetNumJoystickHats(js,1)`

Example: See joysticktest.pbl in the demo directory

See Also: GetNumJoysticks(), OpenJoystick(), GetNumJoystickAxes() GetNumJoystickBalls(), GetNumJoystickButtons(), GetNumJoystickHats() GetJoystickAxisState(), GetJoystickHatState(), GetJoystickButtonState()

Name/Symbol: `GetNumJoysticks`

Description: This gets the number of joysticks available on a system. It returns an integer, which if greater than you can open a joystick using the OpenJoystick() function..

Usage: `GetNumJoysticks()`

Example: See joysticktest.pbl in the demo directory

See Also: GetNumJoysticks(), OpenJoystick(), GetNumJoystickAxes() GetNumJoystickBalls(), GetNumJoystickButtons(), GetNumJoystickHats() GetJoystickAxisState(), GetJoystickHatState(), GetJoystickButtonState()

Name/Symbol: `GetPEBLVersion()`

105

Description: Returns a string describing which version of PEBL you are running.

Usage: `GetPEBLVersion()`

Example: `Print(GetPEBLVersion())`

See Also: `TimeStamp()`

Name/Symbol: `GetPixelColor()`

Description: Gets a color object specifying the color of a particular pixel on a widget.

Usage: `color <- GetPixelColor(widget,x,y)`

Example:
```
  ##Judge brightness of a pixel
  img <- MakeImage("test.png")
  col <- GetPixelColor(img,20,20)
  hsv <- RGBtoHSV(col)
  Print(Third(hsv))
```

See Also: `SetPixel()`

Name/Symbol: `GetPPortState`

Description: Gets the parallel port state, as a list of 8 'bits' (1s or 0s).

Usage: `out <- SetPPortState(pport)`

Example:

See Also: `COMPortGetByte, COMPortSendByte, OpenPPort OpenCOMPort, SetPPortMode, GetPPortState`

Name/Symbol: `GetSize()`

Description: Returns a list of [`height, width`], specifying the size of the widget. The .width and .height properties can also be used instead of this function

Usage: `GetSize(<widget>)`

Example:
```
image <- MakeImage("stim1.bmp")
xy <- GetSize(image)
x <- Nth(xy, 1)
y <- Nth(xy, 2)
```

See Also:

Name/Symbol: GetSubNum()

Description: Creates dialog to ask user to input a subject code

Usage: GetSubNum(<win>)

Example:
```
## Put this at the beginning of an experiment,
## after a window gWin has been defined.
##
 if(gSubNum == 0)
  {
    gSubNum <- GetSubNum(gWin)
  }
```
Note: gSubNum can also be set from the command line.

See Also:

Name/Symbol: GetSystemType()

Description: Returns a string identify what type of computer system you are using. It will return either: OSX, LINUX, or WINDOWS.

Usage: GetSystemType()

Example:
```
## Put this at the beginning of an experiment,
## after a window gWin has been defined.
   if(GetSystemType() == "WINDOWS")
    {
      SignalFatalError("Experiment untested on windows")
    }
```

See Also: SystemCall()

Name/Symbol: GetText()

Description: Returns the text stored in a text object (either a textbox or a label). The .text properties can also be used instead of this function.

Usage: `GetText(<widget>)`

Example:

See Also: `SetCursorPosition()`,   `GetCursorPosition()`, `SetEditable()`, `MakeTextBox()`

Name/Symbol: `GetTextBoxCursorFromClick()`

Description: Returns the position (in characters) corresponding to a x,y click on a text box. The X,Y position must be relative to the x,y position of the box, not absolute. Once obtained, the cursor position can be set with SetCursorPosition().

Usage: `GetTextBoxCursorFromClick(<widget>,<x>,<y>)`

Example:
```
win <- MakeWindow()
tb <- EasyTextBox("Click here to set cursor position"
        ,100,100,win,200,200)
Draw()
WaitForClickOnTarget([tb],[1])
 #get the x and y cursor positions
relx <- First(gClick) - (tb.x )
rely <- Second(gClick) - (tb.y )
tb.cursorpos <- GetTextBoxCursorFromClick(tb,
                                          relx,rely))

Draw()
WaitForAnyKeyPress()
```

See Also: `SetCursorPosition()`,   `GetCursorPosition()`, `SetEditable()`, `MakeTextBox()`

Name/Symbol: `GetTime()`

Description: Gets time, in milliseconds, from when PEBL was initialized. Do not use as a seed for the RNG, because it will tend to be about the same on each run. Instead, use `RandomizeTimer()`.

Usage: `GetTime()`

Example:
```
a <- GetTime()
WaitForKeyDown("A")
b <- GetTime()
Print("Response time is: " + (b - a))
```

108

See Also: `TimeStamp()`

Name/Symbol: `GetVideoModes()`

Description: Gets a list of useable video modes (in width/height pixel pairs), as supplied by the video driver.

Usage: `modes <- GetVideoModes()`

Example: ```
Print(GetVideoModes)
##Might return:
[[1440, 900]
, [1360, 768]
, [1152, 864]
, [1024, 768]
, [960, 600]
, [960, 540]
, [840, 525]
, [832, 624]
, [800, 600]
, [800, 512]
, [720, 450]
, [720, 400]
, [700, 525]
]
```

See Also:       `GetCurrentScreenResolution, gVideoWidth,gVideoHeight`

---

Name/Symbol: `GetVocalResponseTime`

Description:    This is a simple audio amplitude voice key controlled by two parameters *ONLY AVAILABLE ON WINDOWS AND LINUX*.

Usage:          ```
GetVocalResponseTime(buffer,
                     timethreshold,
                     energythreshold)
```

This is a simple function that fairly reliably gets an audio response time. It works by recording audio to a buffer, and computing energy for 1-ms bins. When enough bins (whose number/duration is set by timethreshald) in a row surpass an energy threshold (scaled from 0 to 1, set by energythreshold), recording will stop, and the voice key will return. Reasonable values depend on the amount of noise in your microphone, and the types of vocal responses being made. The return time will lag

109

the detection time a bit, and so using the time it takes for the function to return is an unreliable measure of vocal response time.

It returns a list of three elements:

- Response time (in ms),
- End time (using ms counter),
- Responded flag: either 0 or 1, depending on whether the key was tripped,

If the responded flag is 0, the other two numbers will be as well.

See number-stroop.pbl in the stroop directory of the test battery and testaudioin.pbl in demo/ for examples.

Example:

```
buffer <- MakeAudioInputBuffer(5000)
resp0 <-  GetVocalResponseTime(buffer,.35, 200)
SaveAudioToWaveFile("output.wav",buffer)
```

See Also: MakeAudioInputBuffer(), SaveAudioToWaveFile(),

7.9   H

Name/Symbol: `Hide()`

Description: Makes an object invisible, so it will not be drawn.

Usage: `Hide(<object>)`

Example:
```
window <- MakeWindow()
image1  <- MakeImage("pebl.bmp")
image2  <- MakeImage("pebl.bmp")
AddObject(image1, window)
AddObject(image2, window)
Hide(image1)
Hide(image2)
Draw() # empty screen will be drawn.

Wait(3000)
Show(image2)
Draw() # image2 will appear.

Hide(image2)
Draw() # image2 will disappear.

Wait(1000)
Show(image1)
Draw() # image1 will appear.
```

See Also: `Show()`

7.10   I

Name/Symbol: `if`

Description: Simple conditional test.

Usage:
```
if(test)
{
 statements
 to
 be
 executed
}
```

Example:

See Also:

Name/Symbol: `if...elseif...else`

Description: Complex conditional test. Be careful of spacing the else—if you put carriage returns on either side of it, you will get a syntax error. The `elseif` is optional, but multiple `elseif` statements can be strung together. The `else` is also optional, although only one can appear.

Usage:
```
if(test)
{
 statements if true
} elseif (newtest) {
 statements if newtest true; test false
} else {
 other statements
}
```

Example:
```
if(3 == 1) {
          Print("ONE")
}elseif(3==4){
          Print("TWO")
}elseif(4==4){
          Print("THREE")
}elseif(4==4){
          Print("FOUR")
}else{Print("FIVE")}
```

See Also: if

Name/Symbol: `Insert()`

Description: Inserts an element into a list at a specified position, returning the new list. The original list in unchanged.

Usage: `Insert(<[list]>,<item>,<position>)`

Example:
```
x <- [1,2,3,5]
y <- Insert(x,1,4)
##y== [1,2,3,1,5]
```

See Also: `List()`, `Merge`, `Append`

Name/Symbol: `Inside()`

Description: Determines whether an `[x,y]` point is inside another object. Will operate correctly for rectangles, squares, circles, textboxes, images, and labels. `[xylist]` can be a list containing [x,y], and if it is longer the other points will be ignored (such as the list returned by `WaitForMouseButton()`. Returns 1 if inside, 0 if not inside.

Usage: `Inside(<[xylist]>,<object>)`

Example:
```
button <- EasyLabel("Click me to continue", 100,100,gWin,12)

continue <- 1
while(continue)
{
   xy <- WaitForMouseButton()
   continue <- Inside(xy,button)
}
```

See Also: `WaitForMouseButton()`, `GetMouseCursorPosition`

Name/Symbol: `IsAnyKeyDown()`

Description:

Usage: `IsAnyKeyDown()`

Example:

See Also:

Name/Symbol: `IsAudioOut()`

Description: Tests whether `<variant>` is a AudioOut stream.

Usage: `IsAudioOut(<variant>)`

Example:
```
if(IsAudioOut(x))
{
 Play(x)
}
```

See Also: `IsColor()`, `IsImage()`, `IsInteger()`, `IsFileStream()`, `IsFloat()`, `IsFont()`, `IsLabel()`, `IsList()`, `IsNumber()`, `IsString()`, `IsTextBox()`, `IsWidget()`

Name/Symbol: `IsCanvas()`

Description: Tests whether `<variant>` is a Canvas widget.

Usage: `IsCanvas(<variant>)`

Example:
```
if(IsCanvas(x)
{
    SetPixel(x,10,10,MakeColor("red"))
}
```

See Also: `IsAudioOut()`, `IsImage()`, `IsInteger()`, `IsFileStream()`, `IsFloat()`, `IsFont()`, `IsLabel()`, `IsList()`, `IsNumber()`, `IsString()`, `IsTextBox()`, `IsText()` `IsWidget()`, `IsWindow()`

Name/Symbol: `IsColor()`

Description: Tests whether `<variant>` is a Color.

Usage: `IsColor(<variant>)`

Example:
```
if(IsColor(x)
{
 gWin <- MakeWindow(x)
}
```

See Also: `IsAudioOut()`, `IsImage()`, `IsInteger()`, `IsFileStream()`, `IsFloat()`, `IsFont()`, `IsLabel()`, `IsList()`, `IsNumber()`, `IsString()`, `IsTextBox()`, `IsWidget()`, `IsWindow()`

Name/Symbol: IsDirectory()

Description: Determines whether a named path is a directory. Returns 1 if it exists and is a directory, and 0 otherwise.

Usage: IsDirectory(<path>)

Example:
```
filename <- "data-"+gSubNum+".csv"
exists <-  FileExists(filename)
 if(exists)
   {
    out <-    IsDirectory(filename)
    Print(out)
   }
```

See Also: GetDirectoryListing(), FileExists(), IsDirectory(), MakeDirectory()

Name/Symbol: IsImage()

Description: Tests whether <variant> is an Image.

Usage: IsImage(<variant>)

Example:
```
if(IsImage(x))
{
 AddObject(gWin, x)
}
```

See Also: IsAudioOut(), IsColor(), IsInteger(), IsFileStream(), IsFloat(), IsFont(), IsLabel(), IsList(), IsNumber(), IsString(), IsTextBox(), IsWidget()

Name/Symbol: IsInteger()

Description: Tests whether <variant> is an integer type. Note: a number represented internally as a floating-point type whose is an integer will return false. Floating-point numbers can be converted to internally- represented integers with the **ToInteger()** or **Round()** commands.

Usage: IsInteger(<variant>)

115

Example:
```
x <- 44
y <- 23.5
z <- 6.5
test <- x + y + z

IsInteger(x) # true
IsInteger(y) # false
IsInteger(z) # false
IsInteger(test) # false
```

See Also: IsAudioOut(), IsColor(), IsImage(), IsFileStream(), IsFloat(), IsFont(), IsLabel(), IsList(), IsNumber(), IsString(), IsTextBox(), IsWidget()

Name/Symbol: IsFileStream()

Description: Tests whether <variant> is a FileStream object.

Usage: IsFileStream(<variant>)

Example:
```
if(IsFileStream(x))
{
 Print(FileReadWord(x)
}
```

See Also: IsAudioOut(), IsColor(), IsImage(), IsInteger(), IsFloat(), IsFont(), IsLabel(), IsList(), IsNumber(), IsString(), IsTextBox(), IsWidget()

Name/Symbol: IsFloat()

Description: Tests whether <variant> is a floating-point value. Note that floating-point can represent integers with great precision, so that a number appearing as an integer can still be a float.

Usage: IsFloat(<variant>)

Example:
```
x <- 44
y <- 23.5
z <- 6.5
test <- x + y + z

IsFloat(x)      # false
IsFloat(y)      # true
IsFloat(z)      # true
IsFloat(test)   # true
```

See Also:	IsAudioOut(), IsColor(), IsImage(), IsInteger(), IsFileStream(), IsFont(), IsLabel(), IsList(), IsNumber(), IsString(), IsTextBox(), IsWidget()

Name/Symbol:	IsFont()
Description:	Tests whether <variant> is a Font object.
Usage:	IsFont(<variant>)
| Example: | ```
if(IsFont(x))
{
 y <- MakeLabel("stimulus", x)
}
``` |
| See Also: | IsAudioOut(), IsColor(), IsImage(), IsInteger(), IsFileStream(), IsFloat(), IsLabel(), IsList(), IsNumber(), IsString(), IsTextBox(), IsWidget() |

Name/Symbol:	IsKeyDown()
Description:	
Usage:	
Example:	
See Also:	IsKeyUp()

Name/Symbol:	IsKeyUp()
Description:	
Usage:	
Example:	
See Also:	IsKeyDown()

Name/Symbol:	IsLabel()
Description:	Tests whether <variant> is a text Label object.
Usage:	IsLabel(<variant>)
```

| Example: | ```
if(IsLabel(x)
{
 text <- GetText(x)
}
``` |
| See Also: | IsAudioOut(), IsColor(), IsImage(), IsInteger(), IsFileStream(), IsFloat(), IsFont(), IsList(), IsNumber(), IsString(), IsTextBox(), IsWidget() |

Name/Symbol:	IsList()
Description:	Tests whether <variant> is a PEBL list.
Usage:	IsList(<variant>)
| Example: | ```
if(IsList(x))
{
 loop(item, x)
 {
  Print(item)
 }
}
``` |
| See Also: | IsAudioOut(), IsColor(), IsImage(), IsInteger(), IsFileStream(), IsFloat(), IsFont(), IsLabel(), IsNumber(), IsString(), IsTextBox(), IsWidget() |

Name/Symbol:	IsMember()
Description:	Returns true if <element> is a member of <list>.
Usage:	IsMember(<element>,<list>)
| Example: | ```
IsMember(2,[1,4,6,7,7,7,7]) # false
IsMember(2,[1,4,6,7,2,7,7,7])  # true
``` |
| See Also: | |

Name/Symbol:	IsNumber()
Description:	Tests whether <variant> is a number, either a floating-point or an integer.
Usage:	IsNumber(<variant>)
```

Example:
```
if(IsNumber(x))
{
 Print(Sequence(x, x+10, 1))
}
```

See Also: IsAudioOut(), IsColor(), IsImage(), IsInteger(), IsFileStream(), IsFloat(), IsFont(), IsLabel(), IsList(), IsString(), IsTextBox(), IsWidget()

Name/Symbol: IsShape

Description: Tests whether <variant> is a drawable shape, such as a circle, square rectangle, line, bezier curve, or polygon.

Usage: IsShape(<variant>)

Example:
```
if(IsShape(x))
{
  Move(x,300,300)
}
```

See Also: Square(), Circle(), Rectangle(), Line(), Bezier(), Polygon() IsAudioOut(), IsColor(), IsImage(), IsInteger(), IsFileStream(), IsFloat(), IsFont(), IsLabel(), IsList(), IsNumber(), IsString(), IsTextBox(), IsWindow()

Name/Symbol: IsString()

Description: Tests whether <variant> is a text string.

Usage: IsString(<variant>)

Example:
```
if(IsString(x))
{
 tb <- MakeTextBox(x, 100, 100)
}
```

See Also: IsText() IsAudioOut(), IsColor(), IsImage(), IsInteger(), IsFileStream(), IsFloat(), IsFont(), IsLabel(), IsList(), IsNumber(), IsTextBox(), IsWidget()

Name/Symbol: IsText()

Description: Tests whether <variant> is a text string. Same as IsString().

Usage: IsString(<variant>)

Example: if(IsText(x))
                {
                 tb <- MakeTextBox(x, 100, 100)
                }

See Also: IsString()   IsAudioOut(),   IsColor(),   IsImage(),
                IsInteger(),   IsFileStream(),   IsFloat(),   IsFont(),
                IsLabel(), IsList(), IsNumber(), IsTextBox(), IsWidget()

Name/Symbol: IsTextBox()

Description: Tests whether <variant> is a TextBox Object

Usage: IsTextBox(<variant>)

Example: if(IsTextBox(x))
                {
                 Print(GetText(x))
                }

See Also: IsAudioOut(),   IsColor(),   IsImage(),   IsInteger(),
                IsFileStream(),   IsFloat(),   IsFont(),   IsLabel(),
                IsList(), IsNumber(), IsString(), IsWidget()

Name/Symbol: IsWidget

Description: Tests whether <variant> is any kind of a widget object (image,
                label, or textbox).

Usage: IsWidget(<variant>)

Example: if(IsWidget(x))
                {
                 Move(x, 200,300)
                }

See Also: IsAudioOut(),   IsColor(),   IsImage(),   IsInteger(),
                IsFileStream(),   IsFloat(),   IsFont(),   IsLabel(),
                IsList(), IsNumber(), IsString(), IsTextBox()

Name/Symbol: IsWindow

Description: Tests whether <variant> is a window.

Usage: `IsWindow(<variant>)`

Example:
```
if(IsWindow(x))
{
   AddObject(y,x)
}
```

See Also: `IsAudioOut()`, `IsColor()`, `IsImage()`, `IsInteger()`, `IsFileStream()`, `IsFloat()`, `IsFont()`, `IsLabel()`, `IsList()`, `IsNumber()`, `IsString()`, `IsTextBox()`

7.11 K

Name/Symbol: KaniszaPolygon

Description: Creates generic polygon, defined only by with "pac-man" circles
              at specified vertices.

Usage: KaniszaPolygon(<xypoints>, <vertices-to-show>,
                            <circle-size>, <fgcol>, <bgcol>,
                            <show-edge>)

Example: For detailed usage example, see:
              http://peblblog.blogspot.com/2010/11/kanizsa-shapes.html
              Part of a script using KaniszaPolygon:

```
#Specify the xy points
xys <- [[10,10],[10,50],[130,60],[100,100],[150,100],
        [150,20],[80,-10],[45,10]]

#Specify which vertices to show (do all)
show <- [1,1,1,1,1,1,1,1]

#Make one, showing the line
x <- KaniszaPolygon(xys,show,10,fg,bg,1)
AddObject(x,gWin);   Move(x,200,200)

#Make a second, not showing the line
x2 <- KaniszaPolygon(xys,show,10,fg,bg,0)
AddObject(x2,gWin);   Move(x2,400,200)

#Make a third, only showing some vertices:
x3 <- KaniszaPolygon(xys,[1,1,1,1,1,0,0,1],10,fg,bg,0)
AddObject(x3,gWin);   Move(x3,600,200)
```

See Also: Polygon(), KaneszaSquare()

122

Name/Symbol: `KaniszaSquare`

Description: Creates generic Kanesza Square, one defined only by with "pac-man" circles at its vertices:

Usage: `KaniszaSquare(<size>, <circ-rad>,<fgcol>, <bgcol>)`

KaniszaSquare creates a graphical object that can be added to a window, moved to the proper location, etc. Parameters specify the size of the square, the size of the vertex circles, and the foreground and background colors.

Example: For   detailed   usage   example,   see `http://peblblog.blogspot.com/2010/11/kanizsa-shapes.html`

```
gWin <- MakeWindow()
square <- KaniszaSquare(150,20,MakeColor("red"),
                                MakeColor("green"))
AddObject(square,gWin)
Move(square,200,200)
Draw()
WaitForAnyKeyPress()
```

See Also: `Polygon(), KaneszaPolygon()`

7.12   L

Name/Symbol: `Last()`

Description: Returns the last item in a list. Provides faster access to the last item of a list than does Nth().

Usage: `Last(<list>)`

Example: `Last([1,2,3,444]) # == 444`

See Also: `Nth(), First()`

Name/Symbol: `LatinSquare()`

Description: Quick and dirty latin square, taking on just one list argument.

Usage: `LatinSquare(<list>)`

Example:
```
Print(LatinSquare([11,12,13,14,15,16]))
# Output:
#[[11, 12, 13, 14, 15, 16]
#, [12, 13, 14, 15, 16, 11]
#, [13, 14, 15, 16, 11, 12]
#, [14, 15, 16, 11, 12, 13]
#, [15, 16, 11, 12, 13, 14]
#, [16, 11, 12, 13, 14, 15]
#]
```

See Also: `DesignFullCounterBalance(), DesignBalancedSampling(), DesignGrecoLatinSquare(),      DesignLatinSquare(), Repeat(), RepeatList(), Shuffle()`

Name/Symbol: `LaunchFile()`

Description: Launch a specified file or URI with a platform-specific handler.

Usage: `LaunchFile("filename")`

Example: Example uses:

```
#open google:
LaunchFile("http://google.com")
#Open a .pbl file with text editor:
LaunchFile("test.pbl")
#Open a data directory in file manager:
LaunchFile("data\")
```

See Also: SystemCall()

Name/Symbol: LayoutGrid

Description: Creates a grid of x,y points in a range, that are spaced in a specified number of rows and columns. Furthermore, you can specify whether they are vertical or horizontally laid out.

Usage: LayoutGrid(<xmin>,<xmax>,<ymin>,<ymax>,<culumns>,<rows>,<vertical>)

Example: Example PEBL Program using NonoverlapLayout:

```
define Start(p)
{
   gWin <- MakeWindow()
   gVideoWidth <- 800
   gVideoHeight <- 300

   lab1 <- EasyLabel("LayoutGrid, horizontal",
                     200,25,gWin,24)
   lab2 <- EasyLabel("LayoutGrid, vertical",
                     600,25,gWin,24)
   nums <- Sequence(1,20,1)
   stim1 <- []
   stim2 <- []

   font <- MakeFont(gPeblBaseFont,0,25,
            MakeColor("black"),MakeColor("white"),0)
   loop(i,nums)
   {
     stim1 <- Append(stim1,MakeLabel(i+"",font))
     stim2 <- Append(stim2,MakeLabel(i+"",font))
    }

   layout1 <- LayoutGrid(50,gVideoWidth/2-50,
                        50,gVideoHeight-50,5,4,0)
   layout2 <- LayoutGrid(gVideoWidth/2+50,gVideoWidth-50,
```

```
                                50,gVideoHeight-50,5,4,1)


    ##Now, layout the stuff.

    loop(i,Transpose([stim1,layout1]))
     {
        obj <- First(i)
        xy <- Second(i)
        AddObject(obj,gWin)
        Move(obj, First(xy),Second(xy))
     }


    loop(i,Transpose([stim2,layout2]))
     {
        obj <- First(i)
        xy <- Second(i)
        AddObject(obj,gWin)
        Move(obj, First(xy),Second(xy))
     }


    Draw()
    WaitForAnyKeyPress()
}
```

The output of the above program is shown below. Even for
the left configuration, which is too compact (and which takes a
couple seconds to run), the targets are fairly well distributed.

LayoutGrid, horizontal				LayoutGrid, vertical			
1	2	3	4	1	6	11	16
5	6	7	8	2	7	12	17
9	10	11	12	3	8	13	18
13	14	15	16	4	9	14	19
17	18	19	20	5	10	15	20

See Also: NonOverlapLayout()

Name/Symbol: Line()

Description: Creates a line for graphing at x,y ending at x+dx, y+dy. dx
               and dy describe the size of the line. Lines must be added to

126

a parent widget before it can be drawn; it may be added to widgets other than a base window. Properties of lines may be accessed and set later.

Usage:
```
Line(<x>, <y>, <dx>, <dy>, <color>)
```

Example:
```
l <- Line(30,30,20,20, MakeColor("green")
AddObject(l, win)
Draw()
```

See Also:
```
Square(), Ellipse(), Rectangle(), Circle()
```

Name/Symbol: `List()`

Description: Creates a list of items. Functional version of [].

Usage:
```
List(<item1>, <item2>, ....)
```

Example:
```
List(1,2,3,444) # == [1,2,3,444]
```

See Also:
```
[ ], Merge(), Append()
```

Name/Symbol: `ListBy()`

Description: organizes a list into sublists, based on the elements of a second list. It returns a list of two entities: (1) a condition list, describing what values were aggregated across; (2) the nested list elements. The length of each element should be the same.

Together with Match and Filter, ListBy is useful for aggregating data across blocks and conditions for immediate feedback.

Usage:
```
ListBy(<list>, <conds>)
```

Example:
```
a <- Sequence(1,10,1)
   b <- RepeatList([1,2],5)
   x <- ListBy(a,b)
   Print(x)
#[[1, 2],
#  [[1, 3, 5, 7, 9],
#   [2, 4, 6, 8, 10]]
#]

   Print(ListBy(b,a))
#[[1, 2, 3, 4, 5, 6, 7, 8, 9, 10],
# [[1], [2], [1], [2], [1], [2], [1], [2], [1], [2]]]
```

See Also: `List()`, `[ ]`, `Merge()`, `Append()`

Name/Symbol: `ListToString()`

Description: Converts a list of things to a single string

Usage: `ListToString(<list>)`

Example: `ListToString([1,2,3,444]) # == "123444"`
                 `ListToString(["a","b","c","d","e"]) # == "abcde"`

See Also: `SubString`, `StringLength`

Name/Symbol: `Length()`

Description: Returns the number of items in a list.

Usage: `Length(<list>)`

Example: `Length([1,3,55,1515]) # == 4`

See Also: `StringLength()`

Name/Symbol: `Levels()`

Description: Returns sorted list of unique elements of a list.

Usage: `Levels(<list>)`

Example: `Levels([1,3,55,1,5,1,5]) # == [1,3,5,55]`

See Also: `Match()`, `Filter()`, `Sort()`

Name/Symbol: `LoadAudioFile()`

Description: Loads an audio file supported by the ffmpeg library. It is nearly identical to LoadMovie(), but only works for audio files (.ogg, .mp3, .wav, .aiff, .wma, et.). It creates a movie object, which can then be played using PlayMovie() or StartPlayback() functions. Currently, only supported on Windows and Linux.

The ffmpeg (`http://ffmpeg.org`) library supports a wide range of audio formats, including most .wav, .mp3, .ogg, .flac, .aiff, .wma, and others. Currently, there appears to sometimes

128

be playback problems if the audio stream is not stereo, so be sure to convert your audio to stereo. Also, there appears to be some problems with .flac data formats.

If you have problems with playback, you should verify that your media file loads with another ffmpeg media player.

Usage: `LoadAudioFile(audiofile)`

Example:
```
movie <- LoadAudioFile("instuctions.mp3")
PrintProperties(inst)
PlayMovie(inst)
PausePlayback(insnt)
```

See Also: `LoadMovie(),`   `tPlayMovie(),StartPlayback()`
                `PausePlayback()`

Name/Symbol: `LoadMovie()`

Description: Loads a movie file using the ffmpeg library. It creates a movie object, which can then be played using PlayMovie() or Start-Playback() functions. Currently, only supported on Windows and Linux.

The ffmpeg (`http://ffmpeg.org`) library supports a wide range of video and audio formats, including most .mpg, .avi, .ogg and .mp3 type formats. Audio-only formats should load and play with LoadMovie, but another function, LoadAudioFile(), has been created for these, as they do not need to be added to a window to work.

If you have problems with playback, you should verify that your media file loads with another ffmpeg media player.

For technical reasons, a movie MUST be loaded directly onto a window, and not another widget.

Usage: `LoadMovie(movie,window, width, height)`

Example:
```
movie <- LoadMovie("movie.avi",gWin,640,480)
PrintProperties(movie)
Move(movie,20,20)
Draw()
StartPlayback(movie)
Wait(500) #Play 500 ms of the movie.
PausePlayback(movie)
```

See Also: `LoadAudioFile(),`   `LoadMovie(),`
                `tPlayMovie(),StartPlayback() PausePlayback()`

Name/Symbol: `LoadSound()`

Description: Loads a soundfile from `<filename>`, returning a variable that can be played using the PlayForeground or PlayBackground functions. `LoadSound` only loads uncompressed .wav files, but uses a background mixer to play them with fairly low latency. In contrast, LoadAudioFile can load many different multimedia files other than .wav, and uses a different audio playback mechanism. LoadSound is appropriate for playing stimulus sounds and feedback, whereas LoadAudioFile may be more appropriate for instructions and longer feedback that should be encoded efficiently.

When the file gets loaded, it gets automatically transcoded into a stereo 44100-sampling rate audio stream, regardless of its original playback rate. We have reports that in some cases, this can cause some problems, especially if a mono file gets loaded multiple times in an experiment. If you experience playback problems, try converting your audio to stereo 44100 hz and see if it helps.

Usage: `LoadSound(<filename>)`

Example:
```
woof   <- LoadSound("dog.wav")
PlayBackground(woof)
Wait(200)
Stop(woof)
PlayForeground(woof)
```

See Also: `PlayForeground`, `PlayBackground`, `LoadAudioFile`, `LoadMovie`

Name/Symbol: `Log10()`

Description: Log base 10 of `<num>`.

Usage: `Log10(<num>)`

Example:

See Also: `Log2()`, `LogN()`, `Ln()`, `Exp()`

Name/Symbol: `Log2()`

Description: Log base 2 of `<num>`.

Usage: `Log2(<num>)`

Example:

See Also: `Log(), LogN(), Ln(), Exp()`

Name/Symbol: `LogN()`

Description: Log base `<base>` of `<num>`.

Usage: `LogN(<num>, <base>)`

Example: `LogN(100,10) # == 2`
                   `LogN(256,2) # == 8`

See Also: `Log(), Log2(), Ln(), Exp()`

Name/Symbol: `Lowercase()`

Description: Changes a string to lowercase. Useful for testing user input against a stored value, to ensure case differences are not detected.

Usage: `Lowercase(<string>)`

Example: `Lowercase("POtaTo") # == "potato"`

See Also: `Uppercase()`

Name/Symbol: `Ln()`

Description: Natural log of `<num>`.

Usage: `Ln(<num>)`

Example:

See Also: `Log(), Log2(), LogN(), Exp()`

Name/Symbol: `Lookup()`

Description: Returns element in `<database>` corresponding to element of `<keylist>` that matches `<key>`.

                   If no match exists, Match returns an empty list.

Usage:
```
Lookup(<key>,<keylist>,<database>)
```

Example:
```
keys     <- [1,2,3,4,5]
database <- ["market","home","roast beef",
             "none","wee wee wee"]
Print(Lookup(3,keys,database)))

## Or, do something like this:

data  <- [["punky","brewster"],
          ["arnold","jackson"],
          ["richie","cunningham"],
          ["alex","keaton"]]

d2 <- Transpose(data)
key <- First(data)

Print(Lookup("alex", key, data))
##Returns ["alex","keaton"]
```

See Also:
```
Match
```

Name/Symbol: `loop()`

Description: Loops over elements in a list. During each iteration, `<counter>` is bound to each consecutive member of `<list>`.

Usage:
```
loop(<counter>, <list>)
{
 statements
 to
 be
 executed
}
```

Example:

See Also:
```
while(), { }
```

7.13   M

Name/Symbol: `MakeAttneave()`

Description: Makes a random 'Attneave' figure[1]. An Attneave figure is a complex polygon that can be used as a stimulus in a number of situations. It returns a sequence of points for use in Polygon().

MakeAttneave uses ConvexHull, InsertAttneavePointRandom() and ValidateAttneaveShape(), found in Graphics.pbl. Override these to change constraints such as minimum/maximum side lengths, angles, complexity, etc.

MakeAttneave uses a sampling-and-rejection scheme to create in-bounds shapes. Thus, if you specify impossible or nearly-impossible constraints, the time necessary to create shapes may be very long or infinite.

The arguments to MakeAttneave are:

- size: size, in pixels, of a circle from which points are sampled in a uniform distribution.

- numpoints: number of points in the polygon.

- minangle: smallest angle acceptable (in degrees).

- maxangle: largest angle acceptable (in degrees).

Usage: `MakeAttneave(size,numpoints,minangle,maxangle)`

---

[1](Collin, C. A., & Mcmullen, P. A. (2002). Using Matlab to generate families of similar Attneave shapes. Behavior Research Methods Instruments and Computers, 34(1), 55-68.).

Example:
```
gWin <- MakeWindow()
shape <- MakeAttneave(100,5+RandomDiscrete(5),5,170)
pts <- Transpose(shape)
poly <- Polygon(200,200,First(pts),Second(pts),
                    MakeColor("blue"),1)
AddObject(poly,gWin)
Draw()
WaitForAnyKeyPress()
```

See Also: `MakeImage()`, `Polygon()`, `Square()`

Name/Symbol: `MakeAudioInputBuffer(<time-in-ms>)`

Description: Creates a sound buffer to use for audio recording or voicekey sound input. It is currently very simple, allowing only to set the duration. By default, it record mono at 44100 hz.

Usage: `MakeAudioInputBuffer(<time-in-ms>)`

See number-stroop.pbl in the stroop directory of the test battery for examples.

Note: Version 0.12 seems to have some trouble specifying buffers of different lengths. 5000 seems to work, but others (3500?) may not.

Example:
```
buffer <- MakeAudioInputBuffer(5000)
resp0 <-  GetVocalResponseTime(buffer,.35, 200)
SaveAudioToWaveFile("output.wav",buffer)
```

See Also: `GetVocalResponseTime()`, `SaveAudioToWaveFile()`,

Name/Symbol: `MakeCanvas()`

Description: Makes a canvas object `<x>` pixels by y pixels, in color `<color>`.

A canvas is an object that other objects can be attached to, and imprinted upon. When the canvas gets moved, the attached objects move as well. The background of a canvas can be made invisible by using a color with alpha channel == 0. The Setpixel and SetPoint functions let you change individual pixels on a canvas, to enable adding noise, drawing functional images, etc. A canvas gets 'cleared' by calling ResetCanvas(canvas). Any object added to a canvas creates an 'imprint' on the canvas that remains if the object is moved. This allows you to use

134

another image as a paintbrush on the canvas, and lets you to add noise to text. Because a text label gets re-rendered when its drawn, if you want to add pixel noise to a stimulus, you can create a label, add it to a canvas, then add pixel noise to the canvas.

Usage: `MakeCanvas(<x>, <y>, <color>)`

Example:
```
gWin <- MakeWindow()
clear <- MakeColor("white")
clear.alpha <- 0
#make a transparent canvas:
x <- MakeCanvas(300,300,clear)
AddObject(x,gWin)
Move(x,300,300)
img <- MakeImage("pebl.png")
AddObject(img,x)
Move(img,100,100)
Draw(x)          #imprint the image on the canvas
Move(img,100,200)
Draw(x)          #imprint the image on the canvas
Hide(img)

#draw a line on the canvas
 i <- 10
 red <- MakeColor("red")
while(i < 200)
 {
   SetPixel(x,20,i,red)
   i <- i + 1
 }
Draw()
WaitForAnyKeyPress()
```

See Also: `MakeImage()`, `SetPixel()`, `MakeGabor()`, `ResetCanvas()`

Name/Symbol: `MakeColor()`

Description: Makes a color from `<colorname>` such as "red", "green", and nearly 800 others. Color names and corresponding RGB values can be found in `doc/colors.txt`.

Usage: `MakeColor(<colorname>)`

Example:

See Also: `MakeColorRGB()`, `RGBtoHSV()`

135

Name/Symbol: `MakeColorRGB()`

Description: Makes an RGB color by specifying `<red>`, `<green>`, and `<blue>` values (between 0 and 255).

Usage: `MakeColorRGB(<red>, <green>, <blue>)`

Example:

See Also: `MakeColor()`, `RGBtoHSV()`

Name/Symbol: `MakeDirectory()`

Description: Creates a directory with a particular name. It will have no effect of the directory already exists.

Usage: `FileExists(<path>)`

Example:
```
#create data subdirectory + subject-specific directory
MakeDirectory("data")
MakeDirectory("data/"+gsubnum)
filename <- "data/"+gsubnum+"/output.csv"
```

See Also: `GetDirectoryListing()`, `FileExists()`, `IsDirectory()`, `MakeDirectory()`

Name/Symbol: `MakeFont()`

Description: Makes a font. The first argument must be a text name of a font. The font can reside anywhere in PEBL's search path, which would primarily include the media/fonts directory, and the working directory (where the script is saved).

- style changes from normal to bold/underline, italic.
- fgcolor and bgcolor need to be colors, not just names of colors
- if show-backing is 0, the font gets rendered with an invisible
- background; otherwise with a bgcolor background. (Note: previous to PEBL 0.11, the final argument = 0 rendered the font with non anti-aliased background, which I can see almost no use for.)

Usage: `MakeFont(<ttf_filename>, <style>, <size>,`
                               `<fgcolor>, <bgcolor>, <show-backing>)`

Example: `font <- MakeFont("Vera.ttf",0,22,MakeColor("black"),`
                                 `MakeColor("white"),1)`

See Also:

Name/Symbol: `MakeGabor()`

Description: Creates a greyscale gabor patch, with seven variables:

- size (in pixels) of square the patch is drawn on
- freq: frequency of grating (number of wavelengths in size)
- sd: standard deviation, in pixels, of gaussian window
- angle: angle of rotation of grating, in radians
- phase: phase offset of grating (in radians)
- bglev: number between 0 and 255 indicating background color in greyscale.

Usage: `MakeGabor(<size>,<freq>,<sd>, <angle>,<phase>,<bglev>)`

MakeGabor creates a canvas that can be used like any image. It must be added to the window, placed, and drawn to appear. Typically, it can take several seconds to create a patch of any large size, so it is usually best to create the gabor patches when the test is initiatialized, or save and load images using WritePNG().

Typically, a sd roughly 1/4 to 1/10 the size of size is necessary to avoid vignetting.

Example: `win <- MakeWindow()`
                   `patch <- MakeGabor(80, 0,10,0,0,100)`

```
AddObject(patch,win)
Move(patch,200,200)
Draw()
```

See Also: MakeAttneave(), SetPixel()>, MakeCanvas()

Name/Symbol: MakeImage()

Description: Makes an image widget from an image file. .bmp formats should
                    be supported; others may be as well.

Usage:

                    MakeImage(<filename>)

Example:

See Also:

Name/Symbol: MakeLabel()

Description: Makes a text label for display on-screen. Text will be on a single
                    line, and the Move() command centers <text> on the specified
                    point.

Usage: MakeLabel(<text>, <font>)

Example:

See Also:

Name/Symbol: MakeNGonPoints()

Description: Creates a set of points that form a regular n-gon. It can be
                    transformed with functions like RotatePoints, or it can be used
                    to create a graphical object with Polygon.

                    Note: MakeNGonPoints returns a list like:

                       [[x1, x2, x3,...],[y1,y2,y3,...]],

                    while Polygon() takes the X and Y lists independently.

Usage: MakeNGonPoints(<radius>, <num_peaks>)

138

Example:
```
window <- MakeWindow()
ngonp <- MakeNGonPoints(50,10)
ngon <- Polygon(200,200,First(ngonp),Nth(ngonp,2),
                MakeColor("red"),1)
AddObject(ngon,window)
Draw()
```

See Also: MakeStarPoints, Polygon, RotatePoints, ZoomPoints

Name/Symbol: MakeSineWave()

Description: Creates a sine wave that can be played using the Play() or Play-
                Background() functions. It will create a single-channel sound
                at 44100 bitrate, 16 bit precision.

Usage: MakeSineWave(<duration_in_ms>, <hz>, <amplitude>)

- The first argument specifies how long (in ms) the tone should be.

- The second argument specifies the frequency. Good values range between 100 and 2000.

- The third argument specifies the volume. It should be less than 1.0.

Example:
```
##Make a sound that is 1000 ms, but just play 300 ms
sound  <- MakeSineWave(200, 220, 1000)
PlayBackground(sound)
Wait(300)
Stop(sound)
```

See Also: PlayForeground(), PlayBackGround(), Stop()

Name/Symbol: MakeStarPoints()

Description: Creates a set of points that form a regular star. It can be
                transformed with functions like RotatePoints, or it can be used
                to create a graphical object with Polygon.

                Note: MakeStarPoints returns a list:

                [[x1, x2, x3,...],[y1,y2,y3,...]],

                while Polygon() takes the X and Y lists independently.

Usage:	`MakeStarPoints(<outer_radius>, <inner_radius>,` `                <num_peaks>)`

Example:	`window <- MakeWindow()`
	`sp <- MakeStarPoints(50,20,10)`
	`star <- Polygon(200,200,First(sp),Nth(sp,2),`
	`                MakeColor("red"),1)`
	`AddObject(star,window)`
	`Draw()`

See Also:	`MakeNGonPoints, Polygon, RotatePoints, ZoomPoints`

Name/Symbol: `MakeTextBox()`

Description: Creates a textbox in which to display text. Textboxes allow multiple lines of text to be rendered; automatically breaking the text into lines.

Usage: `MakeWindow(<text>,<font>,<width>,<height>)`

Example:
```
font <-MakeFont("Vera.ttf", 1, 12, MakeColor("red"),
MakeColor("green"), 1)
tb <- MakeTextBox("This is the text in the textbox",
font, 100, 250)
```

See Also: `MakeLabel(), GetText(), SetText(), SetCursorPosition(), GetCursorPosition(), SetEditable()`

Name/Symbol: `MakeWindow()`

Description: Creates a window to display things in. Background is specified by `<color>`.

Usage: `MakeWindow(<color>)`

Example:
```
win <- MakeWindow()
gWin <- MakeWindow("white")
```

See Also:

Name/Symbol: `Match()`

Description: Returns a list of 0/1, indicating which elements of `<list>` match `<target>`

Usage: `Match(<list>,target)`

Example:
```
x <- [1,2,3,3,2,2,1]
Print(Match(x,1))  ##== [1,0,0,0,0,0,1]
Print(Match(x,2))  ##== [0,1,0,0,1,1,0]
Print( Match(x,3)  ##== [0,0,1,1,0,0,0]
```

See Also: `Filter()`, `Subset()`, `Lookup()`

Name/Symbol: `Max()`

Description: Returns the largest of `<list>`.

Usage: `Max(<list>)`

Example:
```
c <- [3,4,5,6]
m <- Max(c) # m == 6
```

See Also: `Min()`, `Mean()`, `StDev()`

Name/Symbol: `Mean()`

Description: Returns the mean of the numbers in `<list>`.

Usage: `Mean(<list-of-numbers>)`

Example:
```
c <- [3,4,5,6]
m <- Mean(c) # m == 4.5
```

See Also: `Median()`, `Quantile()`, `StDev()`, `Min()`, `Max()`

Name/Symbol: `Median()`

Description: Returns the median of the numbers in `<list>`.

Usage: `Median(<list-of-numbers>)`

Example:
```
c <- [3,4,5,6,7]
m <- Median(c) # m == 5
```

See Also: `Mean()`, `Quantile()`, `StDev()`, `Min()`, `Max()`

Name/Symbol: `Merge()`

Description: Combines two lists, `<lista>` and `<listb>`, into a single list.

Usage: `Merge(<lista>,<listb>)`

Example: `Merge([1,2,3],[8,9])  # == [1,2,3,8,9]`

See Also: `[ ]`, `Append()`, `List()`

Name/Symbol: `MessageBox()`

Description: Hides what is on the screen and presents a textbox with specified message, with a button to click at the bottom to continue.

Usage: `MessageBox(<message>,<window>)`

Example:
```
gWin <- MakeWindow()
MessageBox("Click below to begin.",gWin)
```

See Also: `GetEasyInput, EasyTextBox`

Name/Symbol: `Min()`

Description: Returns the 'smallest' element of a list.

Usage: `Min(<list>)`

Example:
```
c <- [3,4,5,6]
m <-  Min(c) # == 3
```

See Also: `Max()`

Name/Symbol: `Mod()`

Description: Returns `<num>`, `<mod>`, or remainder of `<num>`/`<mod>`

Usage: `Mod( <num> <mod>)`

Example:
```
Mod(34, 10) # == 4
Mod(3, 10) # == 3
```

See Also: `Div()`

Name/Symbol: `Move()`

142

Description: Moves an object to a specified location. Images and Labels are
              moved according to their center; TextBoxes are moved accord-
              ing to their upper left corner.

Usage: `Move(<object>, <x>, <y>)`

Example: `Move(label, 33, 100)`

See Also: `MoveCorner()`, `MoveCenter()`, `.X` and `.Y` properties.

Name/Symbol: `MoveCenter()`

Description: Moves a TextBox to a specified location according to its center,
              instead of its upper left corner.

Usage: `MoveCenter(<object>, <x>, <y>)`

Example: `MoveCenter(TextBox, 33, 100)`

See Also: `Move()`, `MoveCenter()`, `.X` and `.Y` properties

Name/Symbol: `MoveCorner()`

Description: Moves a label or image to a specified location according to its
              upper left corner, instead of its center.

Usage: `MoveCorner(<object>, <x>, <y>)`

Example: `MoveCorner(label, 33, 100)`

See Also: `Move()`, `MoveCenter()`, `.X` and `.Y` properties

Name/Symbol: `NonOverlapLayout`

Description: Creates a set of num points in a xy range, that have a (soft)
              minimum tolerance of 'tol' between points. That is, to the ex-
              tent possible, the returned points will have a minumum distance
              between them of `<tol>`. This may not be possible or be very
              difficult, and so after a limited number of attempts (by default,
              100), the algorithm will return the current configuration, which
              may have some violations of the minimum tolerance rule, but
              it will usually be fairly good.

              The algorithm works by initializing with a random set of points,
              then computing a pairwise distance matrix between all points,
              finding the closest two points, and resampling one of them until

its minumum distance is larger than the current. Thus, each internal iteration uniformly improves (or keeps the configuration the same), and the worst points are reconfigured first, so that even if a configuration that does not satisfy the constraints, it will usually be very close.

Internally, the function (located in pebl-lib/Graphics.pbl) has a variable that controls how many steps are taken, called "limit", which is set to 100. For very compacted or very large iterations, this limit can be increased by editing the file or making a copy of the function.

The function usually returns fairly quickly, so it can often be used real-time between trials. However, for complex enough configurations, it can take on the order of seconds; furthermore, more complex configurations might take longer than less complex configurations, which could represent a potential confound (if more complex stimuli have longer ISIs). Users should thus consider creating the configurations when the test is initialized, or created prior to the study and then saved out to a file for later use.

Usage: NonOverlapLayout(<xmin>,<xmax>,<ymin>,<ymax>,<tol>,<num>)

Example: Example PEBL Program using NonoverlapLayout:

```
define Start(p)
 {
   win <- MakeWindow()
   ## Make 25 points in a square in the middle
   ## of the screen, a minimum of 50 pixels apart.
   ## This is too compact, but it will be OK.

   points <- NonOverlapLayout(100,300,200,400,50,25)
   circs <- []
   ##This should non-overlapping circles of radius 25
   loop(i,points)
    {
       tmp <- Circle(First(i),Second(i),25,
                    MakeColor("blue"),0)
       AddObject(tmp,win)
       circs <- Append(circs,tmp)
    }


   rect1 <- Square(200,300,200,MakeColor("black"),0)
   rect2 <- Square(600,300,200,MakeColor("black"),0)

   AddObject(rect1,win)
   AddObject(rect2,win)
   ##Reduce the tolerance: this one should be bettter
   points <- NonOverlapLayout(500,700,200,400,50,15)


   ##This should non-overlapping circles of radius 15
   loop(i,points)
    {
       tmp <- Circle(First(i),Second(i),
                    15,MakeColor("blue"),0)
       AddObject(tmp,win)
   circs <- Append(circs,tmp)
    }
   Draw()
   WaitForAnyKeyPress()


 }
```

The output of the above program is shown below. Even for the left configuration, which is too compact (and which takes a couple seconds to run), the targets are fairly well distributed.

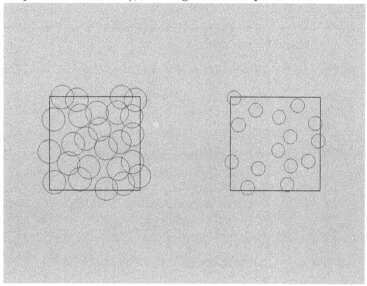

See Also: LayoutGrid()

Name/Symbol: **not**

Description: Logical not

Usage:

Example:

See Also: **and, or**

7.14   N

Name/Symbol: `NormalDensity()`

Description: Computes density of normal standard distribution

Usage: `NormalDensity(<x>)`

Example:

```
Print(NormalDensity(-100))      # 1.8391e-2171
Print(NormalDensity(-2.32635))  #5.97
Print(NormalDensity(0))         #0.398942
Print(NormalDensity(1.28155))   #.90687
Print(NormalDensity(1000))      #inf
```

See Also: `RandomNormal()`, `CumNormInv()`

Name/Symbol: `Nth()`

Description: Extracts the Nth item from a list. Indexes from 1 upwards. `Last()` provides faster access than `Nth()` to the end of a list, which must walk along the list to the desired position.

Usage: `Nth(<list>, <index>)`

Example:
```
a <- ["a","b","c","d"]
Print(Nth(a,3))  # == 'c'
```

See Also: `First()`, `Last()`

Name/Symbol: `NthRoot()`

Description: `<num>` to the power of `1/<root>`.

Usage: `NthRoot(<num>, <root>)`

Example:

See Also:

7.15   O

Name/Symbol: `OpenCOMPort`

Description: This opens a COM/Serial port

Usage: `OpenCOMPort(<portnum>,<baud>)`

Example:

See Also: `COMPortGetByte`,   `COMPortSendByte`,   `OpenPPort`,
                 `SetPPortMode`, `GetPPortMode`

Name/Symbol: `OpenJoystick`

Description: This opens an available joystick, as specified by its index. The
                 returned object can then be used in to access the state of the
                 joystick. It takes an integer argument, and for the most part,
                 if you have a single joystick attached to your system, you will
                 use OpenJoystick(1). If you want to use a second joystick, use
                 OpenJoystick(2), and so on.

Usage: `OpenJoystick()`

Example: See joysticktest.pbl in the demo directory

See Also: GetNumJoysticks(), OpenJoystick(), GetNumJoystickAxes()
                 GetNumJoystickBalls(),   GetNumJoystickButtons(),   Get-
                 NumJoystickHats() GetJoystickAxisState(), GetJoystickHat-
                 State(), GetJoystickButtonState()

Name/Symbol: `OpenNetworkListener()`

Description: Creates a network object that listens on a particular port, and
                 is able to accept incoming connections. You can the nuse
                 `CheckForNetworkConnections` to accept incoming connec-
                 tions. This is an alternative to the `WaitForNetworkConnection`
                 function that allows more flexibility (and allows updating the
                 during waiting for the connection).

Usage: `net <- OpennetworkListener(port)`

148

Example:
```
network <-        OpenNetworkListener(4444)
time <- GetTime()
while(not connected and (GetTime() < time + 5000))
 {
    connected <- CheckForNetwokConnection(network)
 }
```

See Also: CheckForNetworkConnection(),   Getdata(),
              WaitForNetworkConnection(), CloseNetwork()

Name/Symbol: `or`

Description: Logical or

Usage:

Example:

See Also: `and, not`

Name/Symbol: `OpenPPort`

Description: Opens a Parallel port, returning an object that can be used for parallel port communications.

Usage: `OpenPPort(<name>)` The ¡name¿ argument can be one of: "LPT1", "LPT2", and "LPTX". Most likely, a parallel port will be configured to LPT1, but other configurations are sometimes possible.

Example:

See Also: `COMPortGetByte`,   `COMPortSendByte`,   `OpenCOMPort`,
              `SetPPortMode, GetPPortMode`

Name/Symbol: `Order()`

Description: Returns a list of indices describing the order of values by position, from min to max.

Usage: `Order(<list-of-numbers>)`

Example:
```
n <- [33,12,1,5,9]
  o <- Order(n)
   Print(o) #should print [3,4,5,2,1]
```

See Also: `Rank()`

7.16   P

Name/Symbol: `PausePlayback()`

Description: Pauses a playing movie or audio stream. This is used for movies whose playback was initiated using STartPlayback, which then ran as background threads during a Wait() function.

Usage: `PausePlayBack(movie)`

Example:
```
movie <- LoadMovie("movie.avi",gWin,640,480)
PrintProperties(movie)
Move(movie,20,20)
Draw()
StartPlayback(movie)
Wait(500) #Play 500 ms of the movie.
PausePlayback(movie)
Wait(500)
```

See Also: `LoadAudioFile()`,   `LoadMovie()`,   `tPlayMovie()`, `StartPlayback()`

Name/Symbol: `PlayForeground()`

Description: Plays the sound 'in the foreground'; does not return until the sound is complete.

Usage: `PlayForeground(<sound>)`

Example:
```
sound  <- MakeSineWave(200, 220, 1000)
PlayForeground(sound)
```

See Also: `PlayBackground(), Stop()`

Name/Symbol: `PlayBackground()`

Description: Plays the sound 'in the background', returning immediately.

Usage: `PlayBackground(<sound>)`

Example:
```
sound  <- MakeSineWave(200, 220, 1000)
PlayBackground(sound)
Wait(300)
Stop(sound)
```

See Also: `PlayForeground()`, `Stop()`

Name/Symbol: `PlayMovie()`

Description: Plays the movie (or other multimedia file) loaded via either the LoadMovie or LoadAudioFile function. Note that this functionality uses a different underlying system than the sound playing functions PlayBackground and PlayForeground, and they are not interchangeable.

Usage: `PlayMovie(movie)`

Example:
```
movie <- LoadMovie("movie.avi",gWin,640,480)
PrintProperties(movie)
Move(movie,20,20)
movie.volume <- .1
status <- EasyLabel("Demo Movie Player",300,25,gWin,22)
Draw()
PlayMovie(movie)
```

See Also: `LoadAudioFile()`,   `LoadMovie()`,   `StartPlayback()`, `PausePlayback()`

Name/Symbol: `Plus`

Description: Creates a polygon in the shape of a plus sign. Arguments include position in window.

- `<x>` and `<y>` is the position of the center
- `<size>` or the size of the plus sign in pixels
- `<width>` thickness of the plus
- `<color>` is a color object (not just the name)

Like other drawn objects, the plus must then be added to the window to appear.

Usage: `Plus(x,y,size,width,color)`

Example:
```
win <- MakeWindow()
p1 <- Plus(100,100,80,15,MakeColor("red"))
AddObject(p1,win)
Draw()
```

See Also: `BlockE()`, `Polygon()`, `MakeStarPoints()`, `MakeNGonPoints()`

Name/Symbol: `Polygon`

Description: Creates a polygon in the shape of the points specified by `<xpoints>`, `<ypoints>`. The lists `<xpoints>` and `<ypoints>` are adjusted by `<x>` and `<y>`, so they should be relative to 0, not the location you want the points to be at.

Like other drawn objects, the polygon must then be added to the window to appear.

Usage:
```
Polygon(<x>,<y>,<xpoints>,<ypoints>,
        <color>,<filled>)
```

Example:
```
win <- MakeWindow()
 #This makes a T
 xpoints <- [-10,10,10,20,20,-20,-20,-10]
 ypoints <- [-20,-20,40,40,50,50,40,40]
 p1 <-    Polygon(100,100,xpoints, ypoints,
                      MakeColor("black"),1)
 AddObject(p1,win)
 Draw()
```

See Also: `BlockE()`, `Bezier()`, `MakeStarPoints()`, `MakeNGonPoints()`

Name/Symbol: `Pow()`

Description: Raises or lowers `<num>` to the power of `<pow>`.

Usage: `Pow(<num>, <pow>)`

Example:
```
Pow(2,6) # == 64
Pow(5,0) # == 1
```

See Also:

Name/Symbol: `Print()`

Description: Prints `<value>` to stdout (the console [Linux] or the file `stdout.txt` [Windows]), and then appends a newline afterwards.

Usage: `Print(<value>)`

Example:
```
 Print("hello world")
 Print(33 + 43)
 x <-Print("Once")
```

152

See Also: `Print_(), FilePrint()`

Name/Symbol: `PrintProperties()`

Description: Prints .properties/values for any complex object. These include textboxes, fonts, colors, images, shapes, etc. Mostly useful as a debugging tool.

Usage: `PrintProperties(<object>)`

Example:

```
win <- MakeWindow()
tb <- EasyTextbox("one",20,20,win,22,400,80)
PrintProperties(tb)

##Output:
----------
[CURSORPOS]: 0
[EDITABLE]: 0
[HEIGHT]: 80
[ROTATION]: 0
[TEXT]: one
[VISIBLE]: 1
[WIDTH]: 400
[X]: 20
[Y]: 20
[ZOOMX]: 1
[ZOOMY]: 1
----------
```

See Also: `Print()`

Name/Symbol: `Print_()`

Description: Prints <value> to stdout; doesn't append a newline afterwards.

Usage: `Print_(<value>)`

Example:
```
Print_("This line")
Print_(" ")
Print_("and")
Print_(" ")
Print("Another line")
# prints out: 'This line and Another line'
```

See Also: `Print(), FilePrint()`

Name/Symbol: `PrintList()`

Description: Prints a list, without the ','s or [] characters. Puts a carriage return at the end. Returns a string that was printed. If a list contains other lists, the printing will wrap multiple lines and the internal lists will be printed as normal. To avoid this, try PrintList(Flatten(list)).

Usage: `PrintList( <list>)`

Example:
```
PrintList( [1,2,3,4,5,5,5])
##
##  Produces:
##1 2 3 4 5 5 5
PrintList([[1,2],[3,4],[5,6]])
#Produces:
# [1,2]
#,[3,4]
#,[5,6]

PrintList(Flatten([[1,2],[3,4],[5,6]]))
#Produces:
# 1 2 3 4 5 6
```

See Also: `Print(),    Print_(),    FilePrint(),    FilePrint_(),`
                 `FilePrintList(),`

Name/Symbol: `PushOnEnd`

Description: Pushes an item onto the end of a list, modifying the list itself.

                 Note: `PushOnEnd` is a more efficient replacement for `Append()`. Unlike `Append`, it will modify the original list as a side effect, so the following works:

                 `PushOnEnd(list, item)`

                 There is no need to set the original list to the result of PushOn-End, like you must do with Append. However, it does in fact work, and incurs only a slight overhead, so that Append can often be replaced with PushOnEnd without worry.

```
        list <-  PushOnEnd(list, item)
```

Usage: PushOnEnd(<list>, <item>)

Example: list <- Sequence(1,5,1)
              double <- []
              loop(i, list)
              {
                PushOnEnd(double, [i,i])
              }
              Print(double)
              # Produces [[1,1],[2,2],[3,3],[4,4],[5,5]]

See Also: SetElement() List(), [ ], Merge(), PushOnEnd

7.17   Q

Name/Symbol: `Quantile()`

Description: Returns the `<num>` quantile of the numbers in `<list>`. `<num>` should be between 0 and 100

Usage: `Quantile(<list>, <num>)`

Example:
```
##Find 75th percentile to use as a threshold.
thresh <- Quantile(rts,75)
```

See Also: `StDev()`, `Median()`, `Mean()`, `Max()`, `Min()`

7.18   R

Name/Symbol: RadToDeg()

Description: Converts <rad> radians to degrees.

Usage: RadToDeg(<rad>)

Example:

See Also: DegToRad(), Tan(), Cos(), Sin(), ATan(), ASin(), ACos()

Name/Symbol: Random()

Description: Returns a random number between 0 and 1.

Usage: Random()

Example: a <- Random()

See Also: Random(),   RandomBernoulli(),   RandomBinomial(),
RandomDiscrete(),   RandomExponential(),
RandomLogistic(), RandomLogNormal(), RandomNormal(),
RandomUniform(), RandomizeTimer(), SeedRNG()

Name/Symbol: RandomBernoulli()

Description: Returns 0 with probability (1-<p>) and 1 with probability <p>.

Usage: RandomBernoulli(<p>)

Example: RandomBernoulli(.3)

See Also: Random(),   RandomBernoulli(),   RandomBinomial,
RandomDiscrete(),   RandomExponential(),
RandomLogistic(), RandomLogNormal(), RandomNormal(),
RandomUniform(), RandomizeTimer(), SeedRNG()

Name/Symbol: RandomBinomial

Description: Returns a random number according to the Binomial distribution with probability <p> and repetitions <n>, i.e., the number of <p> Bernoulli trials that succeed out of <n> attempts.

Usage: RandomBinomial(<p> <n>)

Example: `RandomBinomial(.3, 10) # returns number from 0 to 10`

See Also: `Random()`, `RandomBernoulli()`, `RandomBinomial`, `RandomDiscrete()`, `RandomExponential()`, `RandomLogistic()`, `RandomLogNormal()`, `RandomNormal()`, `RandomUniform()`, `RandomizeTimer()`, `SeedRNG()`

Name/Symbol: `RandomDiscrete()`

Description: Returns a random integer between 1 and the argument (inclusive), each with equal probability. If the argument is a floating-point value, it will be truncated down; if it is less than 1, it will return 1, and possibly a warning message.

Usage: `RandomDiscrete(<num>)`

Example:
```
 # Returns a random integer between 1 and 30:
RandomDiscrete(30)
```

See Also: `Random()`, `RandomBernoulli()`, `RandomBinomial`, `RandomDiscrete()`, `RandomExponential()`, `RandomLogistic()`, `RandomLogNormal()`, `RandomNormal()`, `RandomUniform()`, `RandomizeTimer()`, `SeedRNG()`

Name/Symbol: `RandomExponential()`

Description: Returns a random number according to exponential distribution with mean `<mean>` (or decay 1/mean).

Usage: `RandomExponential(<mean>)`

Example: `RandomExponential(100)`

See Also: `Random()`, `RandomBernoulli()`, `RandomBinomial`, `RandomDiscrete()`, `RandomLogistic()`, `RandomLogNormal()`, `RandomNormal()`, `RandomUniform()`, `RandomizeTimer`, `SeedRNG()`

Name/Symbol: `RandomizeTimer()`

Description: Seeds the RNG with the current time.

Usage: `RandomizeTimer()`

Example:
```
RandomizeTimer()
x <- Random()
```

See Also: Random(),   RandomBernoulli(),   RandomBinomial,
            RandomDiscrete(),   RandomExponential(),
            RandomLogistic(), RandomLogNormal(), RandomNormal(),
            RandomUniform(), SeedRNG()

Name/Symbol: RandomLogistic()

Description: Returns a random number according to the logistic distribution
              with parameter <p>: f(x) = exp(x)/(1+exp(x))

Usage: RandomLogistic(<p>)

Example: RandomLogistic(.3)

See Also: Random(),   RandomBernoulli(),   RandomBinomial,
             RandomDiscrete(),   RandomExponential(),
             RandomLogNormal(), RandomNormal(), RandomUniform(),
             RandomizeTimer, SeedRNG()

Name/Symbol: RandomLogNormal()

Description: Returns a random number according to the log-normal distri-
              bution with parameters <median> and <spread>. Generated
              by calculating $median*exp(spread*RandomNormal(0,1))$.
              <spread> is a shape parameter, and only affects the variance as
              a function of the median; similar to the coefficient of variation.
              A value near 0 is a sharp distribution (.1-.3), larger values are
              more spread out; values greater than 2 make little difference in
              the shape.

Usage: RandomLogNormal(<median>, <spread>)

Example: RandomLogNormal(5000, .1)

See Also: Random(),   RandomBernoulli(),   RandomBinomial,
             RandomDiscrete(),   RandomExponential(),
             RandomLogistic(), RandomNormal(), RandomUniform(),
             RandomizeTimer, SeedRNG()

Name/Symbol: RandomNormal()

Description: Returns a random number according to the standard normal
              distribution with <mean> and <stdev>.

Usage: RandomNormal(<mean>, <stdev>)

159

Example:

See Also: Random(),   RandomBernoulli(),   RandomBinomial,
RandomDiscrete(),   RandomExponential(),
RandomLogistic(), RandomLogNormal(), RandomUniform(),
RandomizeTimer, SeedRNG()

Name/Symbol: RandomUniform()

Description: Returns a random floating-point number between 0 and <num>.

Usage: RandomUniform(<num>)

Example:

See Also: Random(),   RandomBernoulli(),   RandomBinomial,
RandomDiscrete(),   RandomExponential(),
RandomLogistic(), RandomLogNormal(), RandomNormal(),
RandomizeTimer(), SeedRNG()

Name/Symbol: Rank()

Description: Returns a list of numbers describing the rank of each position,
from min to max. The same as calling Order(Order(x)).

Usage: Rank(<list-of-numbers>)

Example: n <- [33,12,1,5,9]
o <- Rank(n)
Print(o) #should print [5,4,1,2,3]

See Also: Order()

Name/Symbol: ReadCSV()

Description: Reads a comma-separated value file into a nested list. Need not
be named with a .csv extension. It should properly strip quotes
from cells, and not break entries on commas embedded within
quoted text.

Usage: ReadCSV(<filename>)

Example: table <- ReadCSV("datafile.csv")

See Also: FileReadTable(), FileReadList, StripQuotes

Name/Symbol: `Rectangle()`

Description: Creates a rectangle for graphing at x,y with size dx and dy. Rectangles are only currently definable oriented in horizontal/vertical directions. A rectangle must be added to a parent widget before it can be drawn; it may be added to widgets other than a base window. The properties of rectangles may be changed by accessing their properties directly, including the FILLED property which makes the object an outline versus a filled shape.

Usage: `Rectangle(<x>, <y>, <dx>, <dy>, <color>)`

Example:

```
r <- Rectangle(30,30,20,10, MakeColor(green))
AddObject(r, win)
Draw()
```

See Also: `Circle(), Ellipse(), Square(), Line()`

Name/Symbol: `ReflectPoints`

Description: Takes a set of points (defined in a joined list [[x1,x2,x3,...],[y1,y2,y3,...]]   and reflects them around the vertical axis x=0, returning a similar [[x],[y]] list. Identical to `ZoomPoints(pts,-1,1)`

Usage: `ReflectPoints(<points>)`

Example: `points <- [[1,2,3,4],[20,21,22,23]]`
`newpoints <- ReflectPoints(points)`

See Also: `ZoomPoints(), RotatePoints`

Name/Symbol: `RegisterEvent()`

Description: Adds an event to the event loop. This function is currently experimental, and its usage may change in future versions of PEBL.

Usage: `USAGE CURRENTLY UNDOCUMENTED`

Example:

See Also: `ClearEventLoop(), StartEventLoop()`

Name/Symbol: `RemoveFile()`

Description: Removes a file from the file system.

Usage: `RemoveObject( <filename>)`

Example:
```
tmpfile <- FileOpenWrite("tmp.txt")
FilePrint(tmpfile,Random())
FileClose(tmpfile)
text <- FileReadText("tmp.txt")
RemoveFile("tmp.txt")
```

See Also:

See Also: `GetDirectoryListing(), FileExists(), IsDirectory(), MakeDirectory()`

Name/Symbol: `RemoveObject()`

Description: Removes a child widget from a parent. Useful if you are adding a local widget to a global window inside a loop. If you do not remove the object and only `Hide()` it, drawing will be sluggish. Objects that are local to a function are removed automatically when the function terminates, so you do not need to call `RemoveObject()` on them at the end of a function.

Usage: `RemoveObject( <object>, <parent>)`

Example:

See Also:

Name/Symbol: `RemoveSubset()`

Description: Removes a subset of elements from a list. Creates a new list, and does not affect the original

Usage: `RemoveSubset(<list1>,<list-of-element-indices>])`

Example:
```
list1 <- [1,2,2,4,5]
list2 <- RemoveSubset(list1,[2,3])
Print(list1) #[1,2,2,4,5]
Print(list2) #[1,4,5]
```

See Also: `Merge(), Insert(), Rest()`

Name/Symbol: `Repeat()`

Description: Makes and returns a list by repeating `<object>` `<n>` times. Has no effect on the object. Repeat will not make new copies of the object. If you later change the object, you will change every object in the list.

Usage: `Repeat(<object>, <n>)`

Example:
```
x <- "potato"
y <- repeat(x, 10)
Print(y)
# produces ["potato","potato","potato",
            "potato","potato", "potato",
            "potato","potato","potato","potato"]
```

See Also: `RepeatList()`

Name/Symbol: `RepeatList()`

Description: Makes a longer list by repeating a shorter list `<n>` times. Has no effect on the list itself, but changes made to objects in the new list will also affect the old list.

Usage: `RepeatList(<list>, <n>)`

Example: `RepeatList([1,2],3) # == [1,2,1,2,1,2]`

See Also: `Repeat(), Merge(), [ ]`

Name/Symbol: `Replace()`

Description: Creates a copy of a (possibly nested) list in which items matching some list are replaced for other items. `<template>` can be any data structure, and can be nested. `<replacementList>` is a list containing two-item list pairs: the to-be-replaced item and to what it should be transformed.
Note: replacement searches the entire `<replacementList>` for matches. If multiple keys are identical, the item will be replaced with the last item that matches.

Usage: `Replace(<template>,<replacementList>)`

Example:

```
x <- ["a","b","c","x"]
rep <- [["a","A"],["b","B"],["x","D"]]
Print(Replace(x,rep))
# Result: [A, B, c, D]
```

See Also: `ReplaceChar()`

Name/Symbol: `ReplaceChar()`

Description: Substitutes `<char2>` for `<char>` in `<string>`. Useful for saving subject entry data in a file; replacing spaces with some other character.

Usage: `ReplaceChar(<string>,<char>,<char2>)`

Example:

```
x <- ["Sing a song of sixpence"]
rep <- ReplaceChar(x," ", "_")
Print(rep)
# Result:  Sing_a_song_of_sixpence
```

See Also: for list items: `Replace()`

Name/Symbol: `ResetCanvas()`

Description: Resets a canvas, so that anything drawn onto it is erased and returned to its background color. Implemented by resetting the background color to itself:

```
canvas.color <- canvas.
```

The function does not return the canvas, but has the side effect of resetting it.

Usage: `ResetCanvas(<list>)`

Example:

```
#create a canvas, add pixel noise, then reset and repeat.
define Start(p)
{
  gWin <- MakeWindow()
  canvas <- MakeCanvas(100,100,MakeColor("black"))
  AddObject(canvas,gWin); Move(canvas,300,300)
  Draw()
```

164

```
white <- MakeColor("white")
##add pixel noise
j <- 1
while(j < 5)
 {
i <- 1
while(i < 200)
 {
   SetPixel(canvas,Round(Random()*100),
            Round(Random()*100),white)
   i <- i +1
 }
Draw()
WaitForAnyKeyPress()
ResetCanvas(canvas)
Draw()
 j <- j + 1
 }
WaitForAnyKeyPress()

}
```

See Also: +SetPixel()+, +MakeCanvas()+, +Draw()+

Name/Symbol: **Rest()**

Description: Returns the 'rest' of a list; a list minus its first element. If the list is empty or has a single member, it will return an empty list []. This is a very common function in LISP.

Usage: Rest(<list>)

Example:
```
x <- Sequence(1,5,1)
y <- Rest(x)
Print(rep)
# Result:  [2,3,4,5]
```

See Also: Insert()

Name/Symbol: **RGBtoHSV()**

Description: Converts a color object to HSV values. May be useful for computing color-space distances an so on. No HSVtoRGB is currently implemented.

Usage: `RGBtoHSV(<color>)`

Example:

            `x <- RGBtoHSV(MakeColor("red"))`

See Also: `MakeColor(), MakeColorRGB`

Name/Symbol: `return`

Description: Enables a function to return a value.

Usage:

```
define funcname()
{
 return 0
}
```

Example:

See Also:

Name/Symbol: `Rotate()`

Description: Returns a list created by rotating a list by `<n>` items. The new list will begin with the `<n+1>`th item of the old list (modulo its length), and contain all of its items in order, jumping back to the beginning and ending with the `<n>`th item. Rotate(`<list>`,0) has no effect. Rotate does not modify the original list.

Usage: `Rotate(<list-of-items>, <n>)`

Example: `Rotate([1,11,111],1)  # == [11,111,1]`

See Also: `Transpose()`

Name/Symbol: `RotatePoints`

Description: Takes a set of points (defined in a joined list `[[x1,x2,x3,...]`, `[y1,y2,y3,...]]` and rotates them `<angle>` degrees around the point `[0,0]`, returning a similar `[[x],[y]]` list.

Usage: `ZoomPoints(<points>,<angle>)`

Example: `points <- [[1,2,3,4],[20,21,22,23]]`
                    `newpoints <- RotatePoints(points,10)`

See Also: ZoomPoints(), ReflectPoints

Name/Symbol: Round()

Description: Rounds <num> to nearest integer, or if optional <precision>
                 argument is included, to nearest $10^{-precision}$.

Usage: Round(<num>)
                 Round(<num>,<precision>)

Example: Round(33.23)   # == 33
                 Round(56.65)   # == 57
                 Round(33.12234,2)   # == 33.12
                 Round(43134.23,-2) # == 43100

See Also: Ceiling(), Floor(), AbsFloor(), ToInt()

7.19   S

Name/Symbol: `Sample()`

Description: Samples a single item from a list, returning it. It is a bit more convenient at times than ShuffleN(list,1), which returns a list of length 1. Implemented as First(ShuffleN(list,1))

Usage: `Sample(<list>)`

Example:
```
Sample([1,1,1,2,2])    # Returns a single number
Sample([1,2,3,4,5,6,7]) # Returns a single number
```

See Also: `SeedRNG(), Sample() ChooseN(), SampleNWithReplacement(), Subset()`

Name/Symbol: `SampleN()`

Description: Samples `<number>` items from list, returning a randomly- ordered list. Items are sampled without replacement, so once an item is chosen it will not be chosen again. If `<number>` is larger than the length of the list, the entire list is returned shuffled. It differs from `ChooseN` in that `ChooseN` returns items in the order they appeared in the originial list. It is implemented as `Shuffle(ChooseN())`.

Usage: `SampleN(<list>, <n>)`

Example:
```
SampleN([1,1,1,2,2], 5)    # Returns 5 numbers
SampleN([1,2,3,4,5,6,7], 3) # Returns 3 numbers
```

See Also: `ChooseN(), SampleNWithReplacement(), Subset()`

Name/Symbol: `SampleNWithReplacement()`

Description: `SampleNWithReplacement` samples `<number>` items from `<list>`, replacing after each draw so that items can be sampled again. `<number>` can be larger than the length of the list. It has no side effects on its arguments.

Usage: `SampleNWithReplacement(<list>, <number>)`

Example:
```
x <- Sequence(1:100,1)
SampleNWithReplacement(x, 10)
# Produces 10 numbers between 1 and 100, possibly
# repeating some.
```

See Also: SampleN(), ChooseN(), Subset()

Name/Symbol: SDTBeta()

Description: SDTBeta computes beta, as defined by signal detection theory.

Usage: SDTBeta(<hr>, <far>)

Example:
```
Print(SDTBeta(.1,.9))   #.67032
Print(SDTBeta(.1,.5))   #.88692
Print(SDTBeta(.5,.5))   #1
Print(SDTBeta(.8,.9))   #0.918612
Print(SDTBeta(.9,.95))  #0.954803
```

Name/Symbol: SaveAudioToWaveFile

Description: Saves a buffer, recorded using the GetAudioInputBuffer, to a .wav file for later analysis or archive.

Usage: SaveAudioToWaveFile(filename, buffer)

This will save a .wav file of a buffer that was recorded (e.g., using GetVocalResponseTime).

See number-stroop.pbl in the stroop directory of the test battery and testaudioin.pbl in demo/ for examples.

Example:
```
gResponseBuffer <- MakeAudioInputBuffer(5000)
resp0 <- GetVocalResponseTime(gResponseBuffer,.35, 200)
    SaveAudioToWaveFile("output.wav",gResponseBuffer)
```

See Also: GetVocalResponseTime(),
MakeAudioInputBuffer()

See Also: SDTDPrime(),

Name/Symbol: SDTDPrime()

Description: SDTDPrime computes d-prime, as defined by signal detection theory. This is a measure of sensitivy based jointly on hit rate and false alarm rate.

Usage: SDTDPrime(<hr>, <far>)

Example:

```
Print(SDTDPrime(.1,.9))   #2.56431
Print(SDTDPrime(.1,.5))   #1.28155
Print(SDTDPrime(.5,.5))   #0
Print(SDTDPrime(.8,.9))   #.43993
Print(SDTDPrime(.9,.95))  #.363302
```

See Also: SDTBeta(),

Name/Symbol: SeedRNG()

Description: Seeds the random number generator with <num> to reproduce a random sequence. This function can be used cleverly to create a multi-session experiment: Start by seeding the RNG with a single number for each subject; generate the stimulus sequence, then extract the appropriate stimuli for the current block. Remember to RandomizeTimer() afterward if necessary.

Usage: SeedRNG(<num>)

Example:

```
##This makes sure you get the same random order
## across sessions for individual subjects.
 SeedRNG(gSubNum)
 stimTmp <- Sequence(1:100,1)
 stim <- Shuffle(stimTmp)
 RandomizeTimer()
```

See Also: RandomizeTimer()

Name/Symbol: SendData()

Description: Sends data on network connection. Example of usage in demo/nim.pbl. You can only send text data.

Usage: SendData(<network>,<data_as_string>)

Example: On 'server':

170

```
net <- WaitForNetworkConnection("localhost",1234)
SendData(net,"Watson, come here. I need you.")
CloseNetworkConnection(net)
```

On Client:

```
net <- ConnectToHost("localhost",1234)
value <-  GetData(net,20)
Print(value)
CloseNetworkConnection(net)
##should print out "Watson, come here. I need you."
```

See Also: ConnectToIP, ConnectToHost, WaitForNetworkConnection, GetData, ConvertIPString, CloseNetworkConnection

---

Name/Symbol: SegmentsIntersect()

Description: Determines whether two line segments, defined by four xy point pairs, intersect. Two line segments that share a corner return 0, although they could be considered to intersect.

This function is defined in pebl-lib/Graphics.pbl

Usage: SegmentsIntersect(x1,y1,x2,y2,
                               a1,b1,a2,b2)

Example: SegmentsIntersect(1,0,2,0,
                               1,2,2,2)   #0

             #returns 0, though they share (1,0)
             SegmentsIntersect(1,0,2,0,
                               1,0,2,2)
             SegmentsIntersect(1,1,3,1,
                               2,2,2,0)   #1

See Also: GetAngle3, ToRight

Name/Symbol: Sequence()

Description: Makes a sequence of numbers from <start> to <end> at <step>-sized increments. If <step> is positive, <end> must be larger than <start>, and if <step> is negative, <end> must be smaller than <start>. If <start> + n*<step> does not exactly equal <end>, the last item in the sequence will be the number closest number to <end> in the direction of <start> (and thus <step>).

171

Usage: `Sequence(<start>, <end>, <step>)`

Example:
```
Sequence(0,10,3)     # == [0,3,6,9]
Sequence(0,10,1.5)   # == [0,1.5,3,4.5, 6, 7.5, 9]
Sequence(10,1,3)     # error
Sequence(10,0,-1)    # == [10,9,8,7,6,5,4,3,2,1]
```

See Also: `Repeat()`, `RepeatList()`

Name/Symbol: `SetCursorPosition()`

Description: Moves the editing cursor to a specified character position in a textbox.

Usage: `SetCursorPosition(<textbox>, <integer>)`

Example: `SetCursorPosition(tb, 23)`

See Also: `SetEditable()`, `GetCursorPosition()`, `SetText()`, `GetText()`

Name/Symbol: `SetEditable()`

Description: Sets the "editable" status of the textbox. All this really does is turns on or off the cursor; editing must be done with the (currently unsupported) device function `GetInput()`.

Usage: `SetEditable()`

Example:

```
SetEditable(tb, 0)
SetEditable(tb, 1)
```

See Also: `GetEditable()`

Name/Symbol: `SetElement()`

Description: Efficiently alter a specific item from a list. `SetElement` has length-constant access time, and so it can be efficient to pre-create a list structure and then populate it one-by-one.

Usage: `SetElement(<list>, <index>, <value>)`

Example:

```
##Set a random subset of elements to their index:
list <- Repeat(0,10)
 index <- 1
 while(index <= 10)
 {
   if(Random()<.2)
    {
       SetElement(list,index,index)
     }
   index <- index + 1
 }
```

See Also: Nth(), Append(), PushOnEnd()

Name/Symbol: SetFont()

Description: Resets the font of a textbox or label. Change will not appear
              until the next **Draw()** function is called. Can be used, for exam-
              ple, to change the color of a label to give richer feedback about
              correctness on a trial (see example below). Font can alse be set
              by assigning to the object.font property of an object.

Usage: SetFont(<text-widget>, <font>)

Example:
```
fontGreen <- MakeFont("vera.ttf",1,22,
                         MakeColor("green"),
                         MakeColor("black"), 1)
fontRed    <- MakeFont("vera.ttf",1,22,
                         MakeColor("red"),
                         MakeColor("black"), 1)
label <- MakeLabel(fontGreen, "Correct")

#Do trial here.

if(response == 1)
{
SetText(label, "CORRECT")
SetFont(label, fontGreen)
} else {
SetText(label, "INCORRECT")
SetFont(label, "fontRed)
}
Draw()
```

See Also: `SetText()`

Name/Symbol: `SetMouseCursorPosition()`

Description: Sets the current x,y coordinates of the mouse pointer, 'warping'
               the mouse to that location immediately

Usage: `SetMouseCursorPosition(<x>,<y>)`

Example:

```
##Set mouse to center of screen:
SetMouseCursorPosition(gVideoWidth/2,
                       gVideoHeight/2)
```

See Also: `ShowCursor,                    WaitForMouseButton,`
               `SetMouseCursorPosition, GetMouseCursorPosition`

Name/Symbol: `SetPixel(), SetPoint()`

Description: Sets the pixel at x,y to a particular color. It can also be called
               using SetPoint(). SetPoint is primarily useful for images and
               canvases–labels and textboxes get re-rendered upon draw so
               any use of SetPixel will get overwritten when it gets drawn. It
               won't work on windows or shapes.

Usage: `SetPixel(<x>,<y>,<color>)`
               `SetPoint(<x>,<y>,<color>)`

Example:

```
back <- MakeCanvas(50,50)
AddObject(back,gWin)
col <- MakeColor("green")
xy <- [[10,10],[10,11],[10,12],[10,13]]
 loop(i,xy)
 {
  SetPixel(First(i),Second(i),col)
 }
Draw()
```

See Also: `SetPoint, MakeGabor`

Name/Symbol: `SetPPortMode`

Description: Sets a parallel port mode, either "¡input¿" or "¡output¿".

174

Usage: `SetPPortMode("<input>")`

Example:

See Also: COMPortGetByte, COMPortSendByte, OpenPPort OpenCOMPort,
                SetPPortMode, GetPPortState

Name/Symbol: SetPPortState

Description: Sets a parallel port state, using a list of 8 'bits' (1s or 0s).

Usage: `SetPPortState([0,0,0,0,0,0,0,0])`

Example:

See Also: COMPortGetByte, COMPortSendByte, OpenPPort OpenCOMPort,
                SetPPortMode, GetPPortState

Name/Symbol: SetText()

Description: Resets the text of a textbox or label. Change will not appear
                until the next `Draw()` function is called. The object.text prop-
                erty can also be used to change text of an object, by doing:
                `object.text <- "new text"`

Usage: `SetText(<text-widget>, <text>)`

Example:
```
# Fixation Cross:
label <- MakeLabel(font, "+")
Draw()

SetText(label, "X")
Wait(100)
Draw()
```

See Also: GetText(), SetFont()

Name/Symbol: Show()

Description: Sets a widget to visible, once it has been added to a parent
                widget. This just changes the visibility property, it does not
                make the widget appear. The widget will not be displayed until
                the `Draw()` function is called. The .visible property of objects
                can also be used to hide or show the object.

Usage: `Show(<object>)`

Example:
```
window <- MakeWindow()
image1  <- MakeImage("pebl.bmp")
image2  <- MakeImage("pebl.bmp")
AddObject(image1, window)
AddObject(image2, window)
Hide(image2)
Draw()
Wait(300)
Show(image2)
Draw()
```

See Also: `Hide()`

Name/Symbol: `ShowCursor()`

Description: Hides or shows the mouse cursor. Currently, the mouse is not used, but on some systems in some configurations, the mouse cursor shows up. Calling `ShowCursor(0)` will turn off the cursor, and `ShowCursor(1)` will turn it back on. Be sure to turn it on at the end of the experiment, or you may actually lose the cursor for good.

Usage: `ShowCursor(<value>)`

Example:
```
window <- MakeWindow()
ShowCursor(0)
## Do experiment here
##

## Turn mouse back on.
ShowCursor(1)
```

See Also:

Name/Symbol: `Shuffle()`

Description: Randomly shuffles a list.

Usage: `Shuffle(list)`

Example:
```
Print(Shuffle([1,2,3,4,5]))
# Results might be anything, like [5,3,2,1,4]
```

See Also: `Sort()`,   `SortBy()`,   `ShuffleRepeat()`, `ShuffleWithoutAdjacents()`

Name/Symbol: `ShuffleRepeat()`

Description: Randomly shuffles `<list>`, repeating `<n>` times. Shuffles each iteration of the list separately, so you are guaranteed to go through all elements of the list before you get another. Returns a nested list.

Usage: `ShuffleRepeat(<list>, <n>)`

Example:
```
Print(ShuffleRepeat([1,2,3,4,5]),3)
##  Results might be anything, like:
## [[5,3,2,1,4], [3,2,5,1,4], [1,4,5,3,2]]
```

Typically, you will want to flatten before using:

```
list <-  Flatten(ShuffleRepeat([1,2,3], 5))
```

See Also: `Sort()`, `SortBy()`, `ShuffleRepeat()`, `ShuffleWithoutAdjacents()`

Name/Symbol: `ShuffleWithoutAdjacents()`

Description: Randomly shuffles `<nested-list>`, attempting to create a list where the nested elements do not appear adjacently in the new list. Returns a list that is flattened one level. It will always return a shuffled list, but it is not guaranteed to return one that has the non-adjacent structure specified, because this is sometimes impossible or very difficult to do randomly. Given small enough non-adjacent constraints with enough fillers, it should be able to find something satisfactory.

Usage: `ShuffleWithoutAdjacents(<nested-list>)`

Example:
```
Print(ShuffleWithoutAdjacents([[1,2,3],
                               [4,5,6],
                               [7,8,9]])
## Example Output:
## [8, 5, 2, 7, 4, 1, 6, 9, 3]
## [7, 4, 8, 1, 9, 2, 5, 3, 6]

## Non-nested items are shuffled without constraint
Print(ShuffleWithoutAdjacents([[1,2,3],
                              11,12,13,14,15,16]))
## output: [13, 11, 2, 14, 3, 15, 1, 16, 12]
##         [13, 12, 2, 16, 15, 11, 1, 14, 3]
```

```
##              [11, 1, 15, 2, 12, 16, 14, 13, 3]

## Sometimes the constraints cannot be satisfied.
## 9 will always appear in position 2
Print(ShuffleWithoutAdjacents([[1,2,3], 9])
## output: [3, 9, 1, 2]
##         [2, 9, 3, 1]
##         [3, 9, 2, 1]
```

See Also: Shuffle(),   Sort(),   SortBy(),   ShuffleRepeat(),
                 ShuffleWithoutAdjacents()

Name/Symbol: `Sign()`

Description: Returns +1 or -1, depending on sign of argument.

Usage: `Sign(<num>)`

Example: `Sign(-332.1)  # == -1`
                 `Sign(65)      # == 1`

See Also: `Abs()`

Name/Symbol: `SignalFatalError()`

Description: Stops PEBL and prints `<message>` to stderr. Useful for type-checking in user-defined functions.

Usage: `SignalFatalError(<message>)`

Example:

```
If(not IsList(x))
{
 SignalFatalError("Tried to frobnicate a List.")
}
##Prints out error message and
##line/filename of function
```

See Also: `Print()`

Name/Symbol: `Sin()`

Description: Sine of `<deg>` degrees.

Usage: `Sin(<deg>)`

Example: `Sin(180)`
                  `Sin(0)`

See Also: `Cos(), Tan(), ATan(), ACos(), ATan()`

Name/Symbol: `Sort()`

Description: Sorts a list by its values from smallest to largest.

Usage: `Sort(<list>)`

Example: `Sort([3,4,2,1,5]) # == [1,2,3,4,5]`

See Also: `SortBy(), Shuffle()`

Name/Symbol: `SortBy()`

Description: Sorts a list by the values in another list, in ascending order.

Usage: `SortBy(<value-list>, <key-list>)`

Example: `SortBy(["Bobby","Greg","Peter"], [3,1,2])`
                  `# == ["Greg","Peter","Bobby"]`

See Also: `Shuffle(), Sort()`

Name/Symbol: `SplitString()`

Description: Splits a string into tokens. `<split>` must be a string. If `<split>` is not found in `<string>`, a list containing the entire string is returned; if split is equal to "", the each letter in the string is placed into a different item in the list. Multiple delimiters, as well as delimiters at the beginning and end of a list, will produce empty list items.

Usage: `SplitString(<string>, <split>)`

Example: `SplitString("Everybody Loves a Clown", " ")`
                  `# Produces ["Everybody", "Loves", "a", "Clown"]`

See Also: `FindInString()`

Name/Symbol: `Square()`

Description: Creates a square for graphing at x,y with size `<size>`. Squares are only currently definable oriented in horizontal/vertical directions. A square must be added to a parent widget before it can be drawn; it may be added to widgets other than a base window. The properties of squares may be changed by accessing their properties directly, including the FILLED property which makes the object an outline versus a filled shape.

Usage: `Ellipse(<x>, <y>, <size>, <color>)`

Example:
```
s <- Square(30,30,20, MakeColor(green))
AddObject(s, win)
Draw()
```

See Also: `Circle()`, `Ellipse()`, `Rectangle()`, `Line()`

Name/Symbol: `Sqrt()`

Description: Square root of `<num>`.

Usage: `Sqrt(<num>)`

Example: `Sqrt(100)  # == 10`

See Also:

Name/Symbol: `StartEventLoop()`

Description: Starts the event loop with currently-registered events. This function is currently experimental, and its usage may change in future versions of PEBL.

Usage: `StartEventLoop()`

Example:

See Also: `RegisterEvent()`, `ClearEventLoop()`

Name/Symbol: `StartPlayback()`

Description: Initiates playback of a movie so that it will play in the background when a Wait() or WaitFor() function is called. This allows one to collect a response while playing a movie. The movie will not actually play until the event loop is started, typically with something like Wait().

Usage: `StartPlayBack(movie)`

Example:
```
movie <- LoadMovie("movie.avi",gWin,640,480)
PrintProperties(movie)
Move(movie,20,20)
Draw()
StartPlayback(movie)
Wait(500) #Play 500 ms of the movie.
PausePlayback(movie)
```

See Also: `LoadAudioFile()`,   `LoadMovie()`,   `tPlayMovie()`, `PausePlayback()`

Name/Symbol: `StDev()`

Description: Returns the standard deviation of `<list>`.

Usage: `StDev(<list>)`

Example: `sd <- StDev([3,5,99,12,1.3,15])`

See Also: `Min()`, `Max()`, `Mean()`, `Median()`, `Quantile()`, `Sum()`

Name/Symbol: `Stop()`

Description: Stops a sound playing in the background from playing. Calling `Stop()` on a sound object that is not playing should have no effect, but if an object is aliased, `Stop()` will stop the file. Note that sounds play in a separate thread, so interrupting the thread has a granularity up to the duration of the thread-switching quantum on your computer; this may be tens of milliseconds.

Usage: `Stop(<sound-object>)`

Example:
```
buzz <- LoadSound("buzz.wav")
PlayBackground(buzz)
Wait(50)
Stop(buzz)
```

See Also: `PlayForeground()`, `PlayBackGround()`

Name/Symbol: `StringLength()`

Description: Determines the length of a string, in characters.

Usage: `StringLength(<string>)`

Example:
```
StringLength("absolute")     # == 8
StringLength("   spaces   ") # == 12
StringLength("")             # == 0
```

See Also: `Length(), SubString()`

Name/Symbol: `StripQuotes()`

Description: Strips quotation marks from the outside of a string. Useful if you are reading in data that is quoted.

Usage: `StripQuotes(<text>)`

Example:
```
text <- gQuote + "abcd" + gQuote
Print(StripQuotes(text))  ## abcd
Print(StripQuotes("aaa")) ##aaa
```

See Also: `StripSpace()`

Name/Symbol: `StripSpace()`

Description: Strips spaces from the start and end of a string. Useful for cleaning up input and such.

Usage: `StripSpaces(<text>)`

Example:
```
text <-  " abcd  "
Print(StripSpace(text))  ## 'abcd'
Print(StripSpace("aaa")) ## 'aaa'
```

See Also: `StripQuotes()`

Name/Symbol: `SubList()`

Description: Extracts a list from another list, by specifying beginning and end points of new sublist.

Usage: `SubList(<list>, <begin>, <end>)`

182

Example: `SubList([1,2,3,4,5,6],3,5) # == [3,4,5]`

See Also: `SubSet()`, `ExtractListItems()`

Name/Symbol: `Subset()`

Description: Extracts a subset of items from another list, returning a new list that includes items from the original list only once and in their original orders. Item indices in the second argument that do not exist in the first argument are ignored. It has no side effects on its arguments.

Usage: `Subset(<list>, <list-of-indices>)`

Example: `Subset([1,2,3,4,5,6],[5,3,1,1]) # == [1,3,5]`
              `Subset([1,2,3,4,5], [23,4,2]) # == [2,4]`

See Also: `SubList()`, `ExtractItems()`, `SampleN()`

Name/Symbol: `SubString()`

Description: Extracts a substring from a longer string.

Usage: `SubString(<string>,<position>,<length>)`

              If position is larger than the length of the string, an empty string is returned. If position + length exceeds the length of the string, a string from `<position>` to the last character of the string is returned.

Example: `SubString("abcdefghijklmnop",3,5) # == "cdefg"`

See Also:

Name/Symbol: `Sum()`

Description: Returns the sum of `<list>`.

Usage: `Sum(<list>)`

Example: `sum <- StDev([3,5,99,12,1.3,15])       # == 135.3`

See Also: `Min()`, `Max()`, `Mean()`, `Median()`, `Quantile()`, `StDev()`

Name/Symbol: `SummaryStats()`

Description:	Computes summary statistics for a data list, aggregated by labels in a condition list. For each condition (distinct label in the <cond> list), it will return a list with the following entries: <cond> <N> <median> <mean> <sd>

Usage: SummaryStats(<data>,<cond>)

Example:
```
dat <- [1.1,1.2,1.3,2.1,2.2,2.3]
cond <- [1,1,1,2,2,2]
Print(SummaryStats(dat,cond))
```

Result:

```
[[1, 3, 1.1, 1.2, 0.0816497]
, [2, 3, 2.1, 2.2, 0.0816497]
]
```

See Also: StDev(), Min(), Max(), Mean(), Median(), Quantile(), Sum()

Name/Symbol: SystemCall()

Description: Calls/runs another operating system command. Can also be used to launch another PEBL program. Useful to check GetSystemType() before running.

Note that the output of a command-line argument is generally not passed back into PEBL; just the function's return code, which is usually 0 on success or some other number on failure (depending upon the type of failure). Some uses might include:

Usage:
```
SystemCall("text-of-command")
SystemCall("text-of-command","command-line-options")
```

Example:
```
if(GetSystemType() == "WINDOWS")
  {
    x <- SystemCall("dir input.txt")
  } else {
    x <- SystemCall("ls input.txt")
  }
  if(x <> 0)
  {
    SignalFatalError("Expected file ["+
        "input.txt] does not exist")
  }
```

See Also: GetSystemType()

7.20   T

Name/Symbol: `Tab()`

Description: Produces a tab character which can be added to a string. If displayed in a text box, it will use a 4-item tab stop.

Usage: `Tab(3)`

Example:
```
Print("Number: "  Tab(1) + number )
Print("Value: "  Tab(1) + value )
Print("Size: "  Tab(1) + size )
```

See Also: `Format()`, `CR()`

Name/Symbol: `Tan()`

Description: Tangent of `<deg>` degrees.

Usage: `Tan(<deg>)`

Example: `Tan(180)`

See Also: `Cos()`, `Sin()`, `ATan()`, `ACos()`, `ATan()`

Name/Symbol: `ThickLine()`

Description: Makes a thick line between two coordinates. This just creates a polygon object to serve as the line.

Usage:
```
ThickLine(<x1>,<y1>,<x2>,<y2>,
          <size-in-pixels>,<color>)
```

Example:
```
a <- ThickLine(10,10,300,400,20,
              MakeColor("red"))
AddObject(a,gWin)
Draw()
```

See Also: `Line()`, `Polygon()`

Name/Symbol: `TimeStamp()`

Description: Returns a string containing the date-and-time, formatted according to local conventions. Should be used for documenting the time-of-day and date an experiment was run, but not for keeping track of timing accuracy. For that, use `GetTime()`.

Usage: `TimeStamp()`

Example:
```
a <- TimeStamp()
Print(a)
```

See Also: `GetTime()`

Name/Symbol: `ToInteger()`

Description: Rounds a number to an integer, changing internal representation.

Usage:
```
ToInteger(<number>)
ToInteger(<floating-point>)
ToInteger(<string-as-number>)
```

Example:
```
ToInteger(33.332)  # == 33
ToInteger("3213")  # == 3213
```

See Also: `Round(), Ceiling(), AbsCeiling(), Floor(), AbsFloor()`

Name/Symbol: `ToFloat()`

Description: Converts number to internal floating-point representation.

Usage: `ToFloat(<number>)`

Example:

See Also:

Name/Symbol: `ToNumber()`

Description: Converts a variant to a number. Most useful for character strings that are interpretable as a number, but may also work for other subtypes.

Usage:
```
ToNumber(<string)
ToNumber(<number>)
```

186

Example: `a <- ToNumber("3232")`
`Print(a + 1) # produces the output 3233.`

See Also: `ToString(), ToFloat(), Round()`

Name/Symbol: `ToRight()`

Description: Determines whether a point p3 is 'to the right' of a line segment defined by p1 to p2. Works essentially by computing the determinant.

Usage: `ToRight(<p1>,<p2>,<p3>)`

Example:
```
a <- [100,0]
b <- [100,100]
c <- [150,50]
ToRight(a,b,c) # returns 1; true
ToRight(b,a,c) # returns 0; false
```

See Also: `GetAngle() GetAngle3, SegmentsIntersect`

Name/Symbol: `ToString()`

Description: Converts value to a string representation. Most useful for numerical values. This conversion is done automatically when strings are combined with numbers.

Usage: `ToString(<number>)`
`ToString(<string>)`

Example:
```
a <- ToString(333.232)
Print(a + "111")
# produces the output '333.232111'.
```

See Also: `ToString(), +.`

Name/Symbol: `TranslateKeyCode()`

Description: Translates a code corresponding to a keyboard key into a keyboard value. This code is returned by some event/device polling functions.

Usage:

Example:

See Also:

Name/Symbol: `Transpose()`

Description: Transposes or "rotates" a list of lists. Each sublist must be of the same length.

Usage: `Transpose(<list-of-lists>)`

Example:
```
Transpose([[1,11,111],[2,22,222],
           [3,33,333], [4,44,444]])
# == [[1,2,3,4],[11,22,33,44],
#      [111,222,333,444]]
```

See Also: `Rotate()`

7.21 U

Name/Symbol: `Uppercase()`

Description: Changes a string to uppercase. Useful for testing user input against a stored value, to ensure case differences are not detected.

Usage: `Uppercase(<string>)`

Example: `Uppercase("POtaTo")  # == "POTATO"`

See Also: `Lowercase()`

7.22   W

Name/Symbol: `Wait()`

Description: Waits the specified number of milliseconds, then returns.

Usage: `Wait(<time>)`

Example: `Wait(100)`
`Wait(15)`

See Also:

Name/Symbol: `WaitForAllKeysUp()`

Description: Wait until all keyboard keys are in the up position. This includes numlock, capslock, etc.

Usage:

Example:

See Also:

Name/Symbol: `WaitForAnyKeyDown()`

Description: Waits for any key to be detected in the down position. This includes numlock, capslock, etc, which can be locked in the down position even if they are not being held down. Will return immediately if a key is being held down before the function is called.

Usage:

Example:

See Also: `WaitForAnyKeyPress()`

Name/Symbol: `WaitForAnyKeyDownWithTimeout()`

Description: Waits until any key is detected in the down position, but will return after a specified number of milliseconds.

Usage: `WaitForAnyKeyDownWithTimeout(<time>)`

Example:

See Also:

Name/Symbol: `WaitForClickOnTarget()`

Description: Allows you to specify a list of graphical objects in `<objectlist>` and awaits a click on any one of them, returning the corresponding key in ¡keylist¿. Also, sets the global variable gClick which saves the location of the click, if you need it for something else.

Usage:
```
x <- WaitForClickOnTarget(<objectlist>,<keylist>)
```

Example:
```
resp <- Sequence(1,5,1)
objs <- []
loop(i,resp)
{
  tmp <- EasyLabel(i +". ",
          100+50*i,100,gWin,25)
  objs <- Append(objs, tmp)
}
Draw()
click  <- WaitForClickOnTarget(objs,resp)
Print("You clicked on " + click)
Print("Click location: [" + First(gClick) +
      ", " + Second(gClick) + "]")
```

See Also:

Name/Symbol: `WaitForClickOnTargetWithTimeout()`

Description: Allows you to specify a list of graphical objects in `<objectlist>` and awaits a click on any one of them, returning the corresponding key in `<keylist>`. Also, sets the global variable gClick which saves the location of the click, if you need it for something else. The function will return after the specified time limit.

If no response is made by timeout, the text ¡timeout¿ will be returned (instead of the correspnoding keylist element), and gClick will be set to [-1, -1].

This function can also be useful to dynamically update some visual object while waiting for a response. Give timeout some small number (below 50 ms, as low as 1-5), and loop over this repeatedly until a 'proper' response is given, redrawing a timer or other dynamic visual element each time.

Usage: x <- WaitForClickOnTarget(<objectlist>,<keylist>,<timeout-in-ms>)

Example:
```
resp <- Sequence(1,5,1)
objs <- []
loop(i,resp)
{
  tmp <- EasyLabel(i +". ",
          100+50*i,100,gWin,25)
  objs <- Append(objs, tmp)
}
Draw()
click  <- WaitForClickOnTargetWithTimeout(objs,resp,3000)
Print("You clicked on " + click)
Print("Click location: [" + First(gClick) +
      ", " + Second(gClick) + "]")
```

See Also: WaitForDownClick(), WaitForMouseButton()

Name/Symbol: WaitForDownClick()

Description: Will wait until the mouse button is clicked down. Returns the
              same 4-tuple as WaitForMouseButton:

```
[xpos,
  ypos,
  button id [1-3],
  "<pressed>" or "<released>"]
```

              but the last element will always be <pressed>. Useful as a
              'click mouse to continue' probe.

Usage: WaitForDownClick()

Example:
```
x <- WaitForDownClick()
Print("Click location: [" + First(x) +
      ", " + Second(x) + "]")
```

See Also: WaitForClickOnTarget(), WaitForMouseButton()

Name/Symbol: WaitForKeyListDown()

Description: Returns when any one of the keys specified in the argument is
              down. If a key is down when called, it will return immediately.

Usage: WaitForKeyListDown(<list-of-keys>)

Example: `WaitForKeyListDown(["a","z"])`

See Also:

Name/Symbol: `WaitForListKeyPressWithTimeout()`

Description: Returns when any one of the keys specified in the argument is pressed, or when the timeout has elapsed; whichever comes first. Will only return on a new keyboard/timeout events, and so a previously pressed key will not trip this function, unlike `WaitForKeyListDown()`. The `<style>` parameter is currently unused, but may be deployed in the future for differences in how or when things should be returned. Returns the value of the pressed key. If the function terminates by exceeding the `<timeout>`, it will return the string `["<timeout>"]`.

Usage:
```
WaitForListKeyPressWithTimeout(<list-of-keys>,
                               <timeout>,<style>)
```

`<list-of-keys>` can include text versions of many keys. See Chapter 4, section "Keyboard Entry" for complete list of keynames.

Example:
```
x <- WaitForListKeyPressWithTimeout(["a","z"],
                                    2000,1)
if(IsList(x))
{
    Print("Did Not Respond.")
}
```

See Also: `WaitForKeyListDown,`   `WaitForListKeyPress,`
`WaitForKeyPressWithTimeout`

Name/Symbol: `WaitForListKeyPress()`

Description: Returns when any one of the keys specified in the argument is pressed. Will only return on a new keyboard event, and so a previously pressed key will not trip this function, unlike `WaitForKeyListDown()` Returns a string indicating the value of the keypress.

Usage: `WaitForListKeyPress(<list-of-keys>)`

Example: `WaitForListKeyPress(["a","z"])`

See Also: `WaitForKeyListDown, WaitForListKeyPressWithTimeout`

193

Name/Symbol: `WaitForKeyPress()`

Description: Waits for a keypress event that matches the specified key. Usage of this function is preferred over `WaitForKeyDown()`, which tests the state of the key. Returns the value of the key pressed.

Usage: `WaitForKeyPress(<key>)`

Example:

See Also: `WaitForAnyKeyPress()`,   `WaitForKeyRelease()`,
              `WaitForListKeyPress()`

Name/Symbol: `WaitForKeyUp()`

Description:

Usage:

Example:

See Also:

Name/Symbol: `WaitForMouseButton()`

Description: Waits for a mouse click event to occur. This takes no arguments, and returns a 4-tuple list, indicating:

```
[xpos,
 ypos,
 button id [1-3],
 "<pressed>" or "<released>"]
```

Usage: `WaitForMouseButton()`

Example:
```
## Here is how to wait for a mouse down-click

continue <- 1
while(continue)
{
    x <- WaitForMouseButton()
    if(Nth(x,4)=="<pressed>")
     {
         continue <- 0
     }
}
Print("Clicked")
```

See Also: ShowCursor,   WaitForMouseButtonWithTimeout
             SetMouseCursorPosition, GetMouseCursorPosition

Name/Symbol: `WaitForMouseButtonWithTimeout()`

Description: Waits for a mouse click event to occur, or a timeout to be
              reached. This takes a single argument: timeout delay in ms.
              When clicked, it returns a 4-tuple list, indicating:

```
[xpos,
 ypos,
 button id [1-3],
 "<pressed>" or "<released>"]
```

              when not click and timeout is reached, it returns a list:
              `[timeout]`

Usage: `WaitForMouseButtonWithTimeOut()`

Example: `## Here is how to wait for a mouse down-click`

```
continue <- 1
while(continue)
{
    x <- WaitForMouseButtonWithTimeout()
    if(First(x)=="<timeout>")
     {
        Print("time is "+GetTime())
        continue <- 1
     } else {
        continue <- 0
     }
}
Print("Clicked")
```

See Also: ShowCursor,   SetMouseCursorPosition,
             GetMouseCursorPosition

Name/Symbol: `WaitForNetworkConnection()`

Description: Listens on a port, waiting until another computer or process
              connects. Return a network object that can be used for com-
              munication.

Usage: `WaitForNetworkConnection(<port>)`

195

Example: See nim.pbl for example of two-way network connection.

```
net <- WaitForNetworkConnection(1234)
dat <- GetData(net,20)
Print(dat)
CloseNetworkConnection(net)
```

See Also: ConnectToHost,   ConnectToIP,   GetData,
                WaitForNetworkConnection, SendData, ConvertIPString,
                CloseNetworkConnection

Name/Symbol: while

Description: 'while' is a keyword, and so is part of the syntax, not a function
                per se. It executes the code inside the {} brackets until the test
                inside the () executes as false. This can easily lead to an infinite
                loop if conditions are not met. Also, there is currently no break
                statement to allow execution to halt early. Unlike some other
                languages, PEBL requires that the {} be present.

Usage:
```
while(<test expression>)
{
 code line 1
 code line 2
}
```

Example:
```
i <- 1
while(i <= 10)
{
 Print(i)
 i <- i + 1
} # prints out the numbers 1 through 10
```

See Also: loop(), { }

Name/Symbol: WritePNG()

Description: WritePNG() creates a graphic file of the screen or a widget on
                the screen. It can also be given an arbitrary widget. For the
                most part, widgets added to other widgets will be captured fine,
                but sometimes polygons and shapes added to other widgets may
                not appear in the output png.

Usage:

```
x <- WritePNG("screen1.png",gWin)

## Use like this to create an animated screencast
define DrawMe()
 {
   pname <- "fileout"+ZeroPad(gid,5)+".png"
   Draw()
   WritePNG(pname,gWin)
 }

define Start(p)
{
  gid <- 1
  gWin <- MakeWindow()
  img <- MakeImage("pebl.png")
  AddObject(img,gWin)
  while(gid < 100)
   {
     Move(img,RandomDiscrete(800),
              RandomDiscrete(600))

     DrawMe()
     gid <- gid + 1
   }

}
```

See Also: FileWriteTable

7.23 Z

Name/Symbol: `ZeroPad`

Description: Takes a number and pads it with zeroes left of the decimal point so that its length is equal to ¡size¿. Argument must be a positive integer and less than ten digits. Returns a string.

Usage: `ZeroPad(<number>, <length>)`

Example:
```
Print(ZeroPad(33,5))      # "00033"
Print(ZeroPad(123456,6))  #"123456"
Print(ZeroPad(1,8))       #"00000001"
```

See Also: `Format()`

Name/Symbol: `ZoomPoints`

Description: Takes a set of points (defined in a joined list [[x1,x2,x3,...],[y1,y2,y3,...]] and adjusts them in the x and y direction independently, returning a similar [[x],[y]] list.

Note: The original points should be centered at zero, because the get adjusted relative to zero, not relative to their center.

Usage: `ZoomPoints(points,<xzoom>,<yzoom>)`

Example:
```
points <- [[1,2,3,4],[20,21,22,23]]
newpoints <- ZoomPoints(points,2,.5)
##Produces [[2,4,6,8],[10,11.5,11,11.5]]
```

See Also: `RotatePoints(), ReflectPoints`

Chapter 8

Color Name Reference

In PEBL, around 750 colors can be accessed by name, using the MakeColor()
function. Each name or corresponds to a specific RGB value. The following
table provides examples of the particular color names, RGB values, and the
obtained shade produced by PEBL.

Table 8.1: Color Reference

Color Name	Red	Green	Blue	Example
ALICE BLUE	240	248	255	
ALICEBLUE	240	248	255	
ANTIQUE WHITE	250	235	215	
ANTIQUEWHITE	250	235	215	
ANTIQUEWHITE1	255	239	219	
ANTIQUEWHITE2	238	223	204	
ANTIQUEWHITE3	205	192	176	
ANTIQUEWHITE4	139	131	120	
AQUAMARINE	127	255	212	
AQUAMARINE1	127	255	212	
AQUAMARINE2	118	238	198	
AQUAMARINE3	102	205	170	
AQUAMARINE4	69	139	116	
AZURE	240	255	255	
AZURE1	240	255	255	
AZURE2	224	238	238	
AZURE3	193	205	205	
AZURE4	131	139	139	
BEIGE	245	245	220	
BISQUE	255	228	196	
BISQUE1	255	228	196	
BISQUE2	238	213	183	

Color Name	Red	Green	Blue	Example
BISQUE3	205	183	158	
BISQUE4	139	125	107	
BLACK	0	0	0	
BLANCHED ALMOND	255	235	205	
BLANCHEDALMOND	255	235	205	
BLUE	0	0	255	
BLUE VIOLET	138	43	226	
BLUE1	0	0	255	
BLUE2	0	0	238	
BLUE3	0	0	205	
BLUE4	0	0	139	
BLUEVIOLET	138	43	226	
BROWN	165	42	42	
BROWN1	255	64	64	
BROWN2	238	59	59	
BROWN3	205	51	51	
BROWN4	139	35	35	
BURLYWOOD	222	184	135	
BURLYWOOD1	255	211	155	
BURLYWOOD2	238	197	145	
BURLYWOOD3	205	170	125	
BURLYWOOD4	139	115	85	
CADET BLUE	95	158	160	
CADETBLUE	95	158	160	
CADETBLUE1	152	245	255	
CADETBLUE2	142	229	238	
CADETBLUE3	122	197	205	
CADETBLUE4	83	134	139	
CHARTREUSE	127	255	0	
CHARTREUSE1	127	255	0	
CHARTREUSE2	118	238	0	
CHARTREUSE3	102	205	0	
CHARTREUSE4	69	139	0	
CHOCOLATE	210	105	30	
CHOCOLATE1	255	127	36	
CHOCOLATE2	238	118	33	
CHOCOLATE3	205	102	29	
CHOCOLATE4	139	69	19	
CORAL	255	127	80	
CORAL1	255	114	86	
CORAL2	238	106	80	
CORAL3	205	91	69	
CORAL4	139	62	47	

Color Name	Red	Green	Blue	Example
CORNFLOWER BLUE	100	149	237	
CORNFLOWERBLUE	100	149	237	
CORNSILK	255	248	220	
CORNSILK1	255	248	220	
CORNSILK2	238	232	205	
CORNSILK3	205	200	177	
CORNSILK4	139	136	120	
CYAN	0	255	255	
CYAN1	0	255	255	
CYAN2	0	238	238	
CYAN3	0	205	205	
CYAN4	0	139	139	
DARK BLUE	0	0	139	
DARK CYAN	0	139	139	
DARK GOLDENROD	184	134	11	
DARK GRAY	169	169	169	
DARK GREEN	0	100	0	
DARK GREY	169	169	169	
DARK KHAKI	189	183	107	
DARK MAGENTA	139	0	139	
DARK OLIVE GREEN	85	107	47	
DARK ORANGE	255	140	0	
DARK ORCHID	153	50	204	
DARK RED	139	0	0	
DARK SALMON	233	150	122	
DARK SEA GREEN	143	188	143	
DARK SLATE BLUE	72	61	139	
DARK SLATE GRAY	47	79	79	
DARK SLATE GREY	47	79	79	
DARK TURQUOISE	0	206	209	
DARK VIOLET	148	0	211	
DARKBLUE	0	0	139	
DARKCYAN	0	139	139	
DARKGOLDENROD	184	134	11	
DARKGOLDENROD1	255	185	15	
DARKGOLDENROD2	238	173	14	
DARKGOLDENROD3	205	149	12	
DARKGOLDENROD4	139	101	8	
DARKGRAY	169	169	169	
DARKGREEN	0	100	0	
DARKGREY	169	169	169	
DARKKHAKI	189	183	107	
DARKMAGENTA	139	0	139	

Color Name	Red	Green	Blue	Example
DARKOLIVEGREEN	85	107	47	
DARKOLIVEGREEN1	202	255	112	
DARKOLIVEGREEN2	188	238	104	
DARKOLIVEGREEN3	162	205	90	
DARKOLIVEGREEN4	110	139	61	
DARKORANGE	255	140	0	
DARKORANGE1	255	127	0	
DARKORANGE2	238	118	0	
DARKORANGE3	205	102	0	
DARKORANGE4	139	69	0	
DARKORCHID	153	50	204	
DARKORCHID1	191	62	255	
DARKORCHID2	178	58	238	
DARKORCHID3	154	50	205	
DARKORCHID4	104	34	139	
DARKRED	139	0	0	
DARKSALMON	233	150	122	
DARKSEAGREEN	143	188	143	
DARKSEAGREEN1	193	255	193	
DARKSEAGREEN2	180	238	180	
DARKSEAGREEN3	155	205	155	
DARKSEAGREEN4	105	139	105	
DARKSLATEBLUE	72	61	139	
DARKSLATEGRAY	47	79	79	
DARKSLATEGRAY1	151	255	255	
DARKSLATEGRAY2	141	238	238	
DARKSLATEGRAY3	121	205	205	
DARKSLATEGRAY4	82	139	139	
DARKSLATEGREY	47	79	79	
DARKTURQUOISE	0	206	209	
DARKVIOLET	148	0	211	
DEEP PINK	255	20	147	
DEEP SKY BLUE	0	191	255	
DEEPPINK	255	20	147	
DEEPPINK1	255	20	147	
DEEPPINK2	238	18	137	
DEEPPINK3	205	16	118	
DEEPPINK4	139	10	80	
DEEPSKYBLUE	0	191	255	
DEEPSKYBLUE1	0	191	255	
DEEPSKYBLUE2	0	178	238	
DEEPSKYBLUE3	0	154	205	
DEEPSKYBLUE4	0	104	139	

Color Name	Red	Green	Blue	Example
DIM GRAY	105	105	105	
DIM GREY	105	105	105	
DIMGRAY	105	105	105	
DIMGREY	105	105	105	
DODGER BLUE	30	144	255	
DODGERBLUE	30	144	255	
DODGERBLUE1	30	144	255	
DODGERBLUE2	28	134	238	
DODGERBLUE3	24	116	205	
DODGERBLUE4	16	78	139	
FIREBRICK	178	34	34	
FIREBRICK1	255	48	48	
FIREBRICK2	238	44	44	
FIREBRICK3	205	38	38	
FIREBRICK4	139	26	26	
FLORAL WHITE	255	250	240	
FLORALWHITE	255	250	240	
FOREST GREEN	34	139	34	
FORESTGREEN	34	139	34	
GAINSBORO	220	220	220	
GHOST WHITE	248	248	255	
GHOSTWHITE	248	248	255	
GOLD	255	215	0	
GOLD1	255	215	0	
GOLD2	238	201	0	
GOLD3	205	173	0	
GOLD4	139	117	0	
GOLDENROD	218	165	32	
GOLDENROD1	255	193	37	
GOLDENROD2	238	180	34	
GOLDENROD3	205	155	29	
GOLDENROD4	139	105	20	
GRAY	190	190	190	
GRAY0	0	0	0	
GRAY1	3	3	3	
GRAY2	5	5	5	
GRAY3	8	8	8	
GRAY4	10	10	10	
GRAY5	13	13	13	
GRAY6	15	15	15	
GRAY7	18	18	18	
GRAY8	20	20	20	
GRAY9	23	23	23	

Color Name	Red	Green	Blue	Example
GRAY10	26	26	26	
GRAY11	28	28	28	
GRAY12	31	31	31	
GRAY13	33	33	33	
GRAY14	36	36	36	
GRAY15	38	38	38	
GRAY16	41	41	41	
GRAY17	43	43	43	
GRAY18	46	46	46	
GRAY19	48	48	48	
GRAY20	51	51	51	
GRAY21	54	54	54	
GRAY22	56	56	56	
GRAY23	59	59	59	
GRAY24	61	61	61	
GRAY25	64	64	64	
GRAY26	66	66	66	
GRAY27	69	69	69	
GRAY28	71	71	71	
GRAY29	74	74	74	
GRAY30	77	77	77	
GRAY31	79	79	79	
GRAY32	82	82	82	
GRAY33	84	84	84	
GRAY34	87	87	87	
GRAY35	89	89	89	
GRAY36	92	92	92	
GRAY37	94	94	94	
GRAY38	97	97	97	
GRAY39	99	99	99	
GRAY40	102	102	102	
GRAY41	105	105	105	
GRAY42	107	107	107	
GRAY43	110	110	110	
GRAY44	112	112	112	
GRAY45	115	115	115	
GRAY46	117	117	117	
GRAY47	120	120	120	
GRAY48	122	122	122	
GRAY49	125	125	125	
GRAY50	127	127	127	
GRAY51	130	130	130	
GRAY52	133	133	133	

Color Name	Red	Green	Blue	Example
GRAY53	135	135	135	
GRAY54	138	138	138	
GRAY55	140	140	140	
GRAY56	143	143	143	
GRAY57	145	145	145	
GRAY58	148	148	148	
GRAY59	150	150	150	
GRAY60	153	153	153	
GRAY61	156	156	156	
GRAY62	158	158	158	
GRAY63	161	161	161	
GRAY64	163	163	163	
GRAY65	166	166	166	
GRAY66	168	168	168	
GRAY67	171	171	171	
GRAY68	173	173	173	
GRAY69	176	176	176	
GRAY70	179	179	179	
GRAY71	181	181	181	
GRAY72	184	184	184	
GRAY73	186	186	186	
GRAY74	189	189	189	
GRAY75	191	191	191	
GRAY76	194	194	194	
GRAY77	196	196	196	
GRAY78	199	199	199	
GRAY79	201	201	201	
GRAY80	204	204	204	
GRAY81	207	207	207	
GRAY82	209	209	209	
GRAY83	212	212	212	
GRAY84	214	214	214	
GRAY85	217	217	217	
GRAY86	219	219	219	
GRAY87	222	222	222	
GRAY88	224	224	224	
GRAY89	227	227	227	
GRAY90	229	229	229	
GRAY91	232	232	232	
GRAY92	235	235	235	
GRAY93	237	237	237	
GRAY94	240	240	240	
GRAY95	242	242	242	

Color Name	Red	Green	Blue	Example
GRAY96	245	245	245	
GRAY97	247	247	247	
GRAY98	250	250	250	
GRAY99	252	252	252	
GRAY100	255	255	255	
GREEN	0	255	0	
GREEN YELLOW	173	255	47	
GREEN1	0	255	0	
GREEN2	0	238	0	
GREEN3	0	205	0	
GREEN4	0	139	0	
GREENYELLOW	173	255	47	
GREY	190	190	190	
GREY0	0	0	0	
GREY1	3	3	3	
GREY2	5	5	5	
GREY3	8	8	8	
GREY4	10	10	10	
GREY5	13	13	13	
GREY6	15	15	15	
GREY7	18	18	18	
GREY8	20	20	20	
GREY9	23	23	23	
GREY10	26	26	26	
GREY11	28	28	28	
GREY12	31	31	31	
GREY13	33	33	33	
GREY14	36	36	36	
GREY15	38	38	38	
GREY16	41	41	41	
GREY17	43	43	43	
GREY18	46	46	46	
GREY19	48	48	48	
GREY20	51	51	51	
GREY21	54	54	54	
GREY22	56	56	56	
GREY23	59	59	59	
GREY24	61	61	61	
GREY25	64	64	64	
GREY26	66	66	66	
GREY27	69	69	69	
GREY28	71	71	71	
GREY29	74	74	74	

Color Name	Red	Green	Blue	Example
GREY30	77	77	77	
GREY31	79	79	79	
GREY32	82	82	82	
GREY33	84	84	84	
GREY34	87	87	87	
GREY35	89	89	89	
GREY36	92	92	92	
GREY37	94	94	94	
GREY38	97	97	97	
GREY39	99	99	99	
GREY40	102	102	102	
GREY41	105	105	105	
GREY42	107	107	107	
GREY43	110	110	110	
GREY44	112	112	112	
GREY45	115	115	115	
GREY46	117	117	117	
GREY47	120	120	120	
GREY48	122	122	122	
GREY49	125	125	125	
GREY50	127	127	127	
GREY51	130	130	130	
GREY52	133	133	133	
GREY53	135	135	135	
GREY54	138	138	138	
GREY55	140	140	140	
GREY56	143	143	143	
GREY57	145	145	145	
GREY58	148	148	148	
GREY59	150	150	150	
GREY60	153	153	153	
GREY61	156	156	156	
GREY62	158	158	158	
GREY63	161	161	161	
GREY64	163	163	163	
GREY65	166	166	166	
GREY66	168	168	168	
GREY67	171	171	171	
GREY68	173	173	173	
GREY69	176	176	176	
GREY70	179	179	179	
GREY71	181	181	181	
GREY72	184	184	184	

Color Name	Red	Green	Blue	Example
GREY73	186	186	186	
GREY74	189	189	189	
GREY75	191	191	191	
GREY76	194	194	194	
GREY77	196	196	196	
GREY78	199	199	199	
GREY79	201	201	201	
GREY80	204	204	204	
GREY81	207	207	207	
GREY82	209	209	209	
GREY83	212	212	212	
GREY84	214	214	214	
GREY85	217	217	217	
GREY86	219	219	219	
GREY87	222	222	222	
GREY88	224	224	224	
GREY89	227	227	227	
GREY90	229	229	229	
GREY91	232	232	232	
GREY92	235	235	235	
GREY93	237	237	237	
GREY94	240	240	240	
GREY95	242	242	242	
GREY96	245	245	245	
GREY97	247	247	247	
GREY98	250	250	250	
GREY99	252	252	252	
GREY100	255	255	255	
HONEYDEW	240	255	240	
HONEYDEW1	240	255	240	
HONEYDEW2	224	238	224	
HONEYDEW3	193	205	193	
HONEYDEW4	131	139	131	
HOT PINK	255	105	180	
HOTPINK	255	105	180	
HOTPINK1	255	110	180	
HOTPINK2	238	106	167	
HOTPINK3	205	96	144	
HOTPINK4	139	58	98	
INDIAN RED	205	92	92	
INDIANRED	205	92	92	
INDIANRED1	255	106	106	
INDIANRED2	238	99	99	

Color Name	Red	Green	Blue	Example
INDIANRED3	205	85	85	
INDIANRED4	139	58	58	
IVORY	255	255	240	
IVORY1	255	255	240	
IVORY2	238	238	224	
IVORY3	205	205	193	
IVORY4	139	139	131	
KHAKI	240	230	140	
KHAKI1	255	246	143	
KHAKI2	238	230	133	
KHAKI3	205	198	115	
KHAKI4	139	134	78	
LAVENDER	230	230	250	
LAVENDER BLUSH	255	240	245	
LAVENDERBLUSH	255	240	245	
LAVENDERBLUSH1	255	240	245	
LAVENDERBLUSH2	238	224	229	
LAVENDERBLUSH3	205	193	197	
LAVENDERBLUSH4	139	131	134	
LAWN GREEN	124	252	0	
LAWNGREEN	124	252	0	
LEMON CHIFFON	255	250	205	
LEMONCHIFFON	255	250	205	
LEMONCHIFFON1	255	250	205	
LEMONCHIFFON2	238	233	191	
LEMONCHIFFON3	205	201	165	
LEMONCHIFFON4	139	137	112	
LIGHT BLUE	173	216	230	
LIGHT CORAL	240	128	128	
LIGHT CYAN	224	255	255	
LIGHT GOLDENROD YELLOW	250	250	210	
LIGHT GOLDENROD	238	221	130	
LIGHT GRAY	211	211	211	
LIGHT GREEN	144	238	144	
LIGHT GREY	211	211	211	
LIGHT PINK	255	182	193	
LIGHT SALMON	255	160	122	
LIGHT SEA GREEN	32	178	170	
LIGHT SKY BLUE	135	206	250	
LIGHT SLATE BLUE	132	112	255	
LIGHT SLATE GRAY	119	136	153	
LIGHT SLATE GREY	119	136	153	
LIGHT STEEL BLUE	176	196	222	

Color Name	Red	Green	Blue	Example
LIGHT YELLOW	255	255	224	
LIGHTBLUE	173	216	230	
LIGHTBLUE1	191	239	255	
LIGHTBLUE2	178	223	238	
LIGHTBLUE3	154	192	205	
LIGHTBLUE4	104	131	139	
LIGHTCORAL	240	128	128	
LIGHTCYAN	224	255	255	
LIGHTCYAN1	224	255	255	
LIGHTCYAN2	209	238	238	
LIGHTCYAN3	180	205	205	
LIGHTCYAN4	122	139	139	
LIGHTGOLDENROD	238	221	130	
LIGHTGOLDENROD1	255	236	139	
LIGHTGOLDENROD2	238	220	130	
LIGHTGOLDENROD3	205	190	112	
LIGHTGOLDENROD4	139	129	76	
LIGHTGOLDENRODYELLOW	250	250	210	
LIGHTGRAY	211	211	211	
LIGHTGREEN	144	238	144	
LIGHTGREY	211	211	211	
LIGHTPINK	255	182	193	
LIGHTPINK1	255	174	185	
LIGHTPINK2	238	162	173	
LIGHTPINK3	205	140	149	
LIGHTPINK4	139	95	101	
LIGHTSALMON	255	160	122	
LIGHTSALMON1	255	160	122	
LIGHTSALMON2	238	149	114	
LIGHTSALMON3	205	129	98	
LIGHTSALMON4	139	87	66	
LIGHTSEAGREEN	32	178	170	
LIGHTSKYBLUE	135	206	250	
LIGHTSKYBLUE1	176	226	255	
LIGHTSKYBLUE2	164	211	238	
LIGHTSKYBLUE3	141	182	205	
LIGHTSKYBLUE4	96	123	139	
LIGHTSLATEBLUE	132	112	255	
LIGHTSLATEGRAY	119	136	153	
LIGHTSLATEGREY	119	136	153	
LIGHTSTEELBLUE	176	196	222	
LIGHTSTEELBLUE1	202	225	255	
LIGHTSTEELBLUE2	188	210	238	

Color Name	Red	Green	Blue	Example
LIGHTSTEELBLUE3	162	181	205	
LIGHTSTEELBLUE4	110	123	139	
LIGHTYELLOW	255	255	224	
LIGHTYELLOW1	255	255	224	
LIGHTYELLOW2	238	238	209	
LIGHTYELLOW3	205	205	180	
LIGHTYELLOW4	139	139	122	
LIME GREEN	50	205	50	
LIMEGREEN	50	205	50	
LINEN	250	240	230	
MAGENTA	255	0	255	
MAGENTA1	255	0	255	
MAGENTA2	238	0	238	
MAGENTA3	205	0	205	
MAGENTA4	139	0	139	
MAROON	176	48	96	
MAROON1	255	52	179	
MAROON2	238	48	167	
MAROON3	205	41	144	
MAROON4	139	28	98	
MEDIUM AQUAMARINE	102	205	170	
MEDIUM BLUE	0	0	205	
MEDIUM ORCHID	186	85	211	
MEDIUM PURPLE	147	112	219	
MEDIUM SEA GREEN	60	179	113	
MEDIUM SLATE BLUE	123	104	238	
MEDIUM SPRING GREEN	0	250	154	
MEDIUM TURQUOISE	72	209	204	
MEDIUM VIOLET RED	199	21	133	
MEDIUMAQUAMARINE	102	205	170	
MEDIUMBLUE	0	0	205	
MEDIUMORCHID	186	85	211	
MEDIUMORCHID1	224	102	255	
MEDIUMORCHID2	209	95	238	
MEDIUMORCHID3	180	82	205	
MEDIUMORCHID4	122	55	139	
MEDIUMPURPLE	147	112	219	
MEDIUMPURPLE1	171	130	255	
MEDIUMPURPLE2	159	121	238	
MEDIUMPURPLE3	137	104	205	
MEDIUMPURPLE4	93	71	139	
MEDIUMSEAGREEN	60	179	113	
MEDIUMSLATEBLUE	123	104	238	

Color Name	Red	Green	Blue	Example
MEDIUMSPRINGGREEN	0	250	154	
MEDIUMTURQUOISE	72	209	204	
MEDIUMVIOLETRED	199	21	133	
MIDNIGHT BLUE	25	25	112	
MIDNIGHTBLUE	25	25	112	
MINT CREAM	245	255	250	
MINTCREAM	245	255	250	
MISTY ROSE	255	228	225	
MISTYROSE	255	228	225	
MISTYROSE1	255	228	225	
MISTYROSE2	238	213	210	
MISTYROSE3	205	183	181	
MISTYROSE4	139	125	123	
MOCCASIN	255	228	181	
NAVAJO WHITE	255	222	173	
NAVAJOWHITE	255	222	173	
NAVAJOWHITE1	255	222	173	
NAVAJOWHITE2	238	207	161	
NAVAJOWHITE3	205	179	139	
NAVAJOWHITE4	139	121	94	
NAVY	0	0	128	
NAVY BLUE	0	0	128	
NAVYBLUE	0	0	128	
OLD LACE	253	245	230	
OLDLACE	253	245	230	
OLIVE DRAB	107	142	35	
OLIVEDRAB	107	142	35	
OLIVEDRAB1	192	255	62	
OLIVEDRAB2	179	238	58	
OLIVEDRAB3	154	205	50	
OLIVEDRAB4	105	139	34	
ORANGE	255	165	0	
ORANGE RED	255	69	0	
ORANGE1	255	165	0	
ORANGE2	238	154	0	
ORANGE3	205	133	0	
ORANGE4	139	90	0	
ORANGERED	255	69	0	
ORANGERED1	255	69	0	
ORANGERED2	238	64	0	
ORANGERED3	205	55	0	
ORANGERED4	139	37	0	
ORCHID	218	112	214	

Color Name	Red	Green	Blue	Example
ORCHID1	255	131	250	
ORCHID2	238	122	233	
ORCHID3	205	105	201	
ORCHID4	139	71	137	
PALE GOLDENROD	238	232	170	
PALE GREEN	152	251	152	
PALE TURQUOISE	175	238	238	
PALE VIOLET RED	219	112	147	
PALEGOLDENROD	238	232	170	
PALEGREEN	152	251	152	
PALEGREEN1	154	255	154	
PALEGREEN2	144	238	144	
PALEGREEN3	124	205	124	
PALEGREEN4	84	139	84	
PALETURQUOISE	175	238	238	
PALETURQUOISE1	187	255	255	
PALETURQUOISE2	174	238	238	
PALETURQUOISE3	150	205	205	
PALETURQUOISE4	102	139	139	
PALEVIOLETRED	219	112	147	
PALEVIOLETRED1	255	130	171	
PALEVIOLETRED2	238	121	159	
PALEVIOLETRED3	205	104	137	
PALEVIOLETRED4	139	71	93	
PAPAYA WHIP	255	239	213	
PAPAYAWHIP	255	239	213	
PEACH PUFF	255	218	185	
PEACHPUFF	255	218	185	
PEACHPUFF1	255	218	185	
PEACHPUFF2	238	203	173	
PEACHPUFF3	205	175	149	
PEACHPUFF4	139	119	101	
PERU	205	133	63	
PINK	255	192	203	
PINK1	255	181	197	
PINK2	238	169	184	
PINK3	205	145	158	
PINK4	139	99	108	
PLUM	221	160	221	
PLUM1	255	187	255	
PLUM2	238	174	238	
PLUM3	205	150	205	
PLUM4	139	102	139	

Color Name	Red	Green	Blue	Example
POWDER BLUE	176	224	230	
POWDERBLUE	176	224	230	
PURPLE	160	32	240	
PURPLE1	155	48	255	
PURPLE2	145	44	238	
PURPLE3	125	38	205	
PURPLE4	85	26	139	
RED	255	0	0	
RED1	255	0	0	
RED2	238	0	0	
RED3	205	0	0	
RED4	139	0	0	
ROSY BROWN	188	143	143	
ROSYBROWN	188	143	143	
ROSYBROWN1	255	193	193	
ROSYBROWN2	238	180	180	
ROSYBROWN3	205	155	155	
ROSYBROWN4	139	105	105	
ROYAL BLUE	65	105	225	
ROYALBLUE	65	105	225	
ROYALBLUE1	72	118	255	
ROYALBLUE2	67	110	238	
ROYALBLUE3	58	95	205	
ROYALBLUE4	39	64	139	
SADDLE BROWN	139	69	19	
SADDLEBROWN	139	69	19	
SALMON	250	128	114	
SALMON1	255	140	105	
SALMON2	238	130	98	
SALMON3	205	112	84	
SALMON4	139	76	57	
SANDY BROWN	244	164	96	
SANDYBROWN	244	164	96	
SEA GREEN	46	139	87	
SEAGREEN	46	139	87	
SEAGREEN1	84	255	159	
SEAGREEN2	78	238	148	
SEAGREEN3	67	205	128	
SEAGREEN4	46	139	87	
SEASHELL	255	245	238	
SEASHELL1	255	245	238	
SEASHELL2	238	229	222	
SEASHELL3	205	197	191	

Color Name	Red	Green	Blue	Example
SEASHELL4	139	134	130	
SIENNA	160	82	45	
SIENNA1	255	130	71	
SIENNA2	238	121	66	
SIENNA3	205	104	57	
SIENNA4	139	71	38	
SKY BLUE	135	206	235	
SKYBLUE	135	206	235	
SKYBLUE1	135	206	255	
SKYBLUE2	126	192	238	
SKYBLUE3	108	166	205	
SKYBLUE4	74	112	139	
SLATE BLUE	106	90	205	
SLATE GRAY	112	128	144	
SLATE GREY	112	128	144	
SLATEBLUE	106	90	205	
SLATEBLUE1	131	111	255	
SLATEBLUE2	122	103	238	
SLATEBLUE3	105	89	205	
SLATEBLUE4	71	60	139	
SLATEGRAY	112	128	144	
SLATEGRAY1	198	226	255	
SLATEGRAY2	185	211	238	
SLATEGRAY3	159	182	205	
SLATEGRAY4	108	123	139	
SLATEGREY	112	128	144	
SNOW	255	250	250	
SNOW1	255	250	250	
SNOW2	238	233	233	
SNOW3	205	201	201	
SNOW4	139	137	137	
SPRING GREEN	0	255	127	
SPRINGGREEN	0	255	127	
SPRINGGREEN1	0	255	127	
SPRINGGREEN2	0	238	118	
SPRINGGREEN3	0	205	102	
SPRINGGREEN4	0	139	69	
STEEL BLUE	70	130	180	
STEELBLUE	70	130	180	
STEELBLUE1	99	184	255	
STEELBLUE2	92	172	238	
STEELBLUE3	79	148	205	
STEELBLUE4	54	100	139	

Color Name	Red	Green	Blue	Example
TAN	210	180	140	
TAN1	255	165	79	
TAN2	238	154	73	
TAN3	205	133	63	
TAN4	139	90	43	
THISTLE	216	191	216	
THISTLE1	255	225	255	
THISTLE2	238	210	238	
THISTLE3	205	181	205	
THISTLE4	139	123	139	
TOMATO	255	99	71	
TOMATO1	255	99	71	
TOMATO2	238	92	66	
TOMATO3	205	79	57	
TOMATO4	139	54	38	
TURQUOISE	64	224	208	
TURQUOISE1	0	245	255	
TURQUOISE2	0	229	238	
TURQUOISE3	0	197	205	
TURQUOISE4	0	134	139	
VIOLET	238	130	238	
VIOLET RED	208	32	144	
VIOLETRED	208	32	144	
VIOLETRED1	255	62	150	
VIOLETRED2	238	58	140	
VIOLETRED3	205	50	120	
VIOLETRED4	139	34	82	
WHEAT	245	222	179	
WHEAT1	255	231	186	
WHEAT2	238	216	174	
WHEAT3	205	186	150	
WHEAT4	139	126	102	
WHITE	255	255	255	
WHITE SMOKE	245	245	245	
WHITESMOKE	245	245	245	
YELLOW	255	255	0	
YELLOW GREEN	154	205	50	
YELLOW1	255	255	0	
YELLOW2	238	238	0	
YELLOW3	205	205	0	
YELLOW4	139	139	0	
YELLOWGREEN	154	205	50	